Dressmaking
SKIRTS & DRESSES

Dressmaking
SKIRTS & DRESSES
A handy step-by-step guide

Alison Smith

LONDON, NEW YORK, MELBOURNE,
MUNICH, DELHI

Project Editor Elizabeth Yeates
Senior Art Editor Elaine Hewson
Managing Editor Penny Smith
Senior Managing Art Editor Marianne Markham
Producer, Pre-Production Rebecca Fallowfield
Senior Producer Katherine Whyte
Special Sales Creative Project Manager Alison Donovan

DK INDIA
Editors Janashree Singha, Manasvi Vohra
Senior Art Editor Balwant Singh
Art Editor Zaurin Thoidingjam
Assistant Art Editor Nikita Sodhi
DTP Designer Satish Chandra Gaur

First published in Great Britain in 2014
by Dorling Kindersley Limited
80 Strand, London WC2R 0RL

Material in this publication was previously published in:
Dressmaking (2012)

A Penguin Random House Company

ISBN 978-1-4093-6971-4

Printed and bound in China by Leo Paper Products Ltd.

Discover more at **www.dk.com/crafts**

CONTENTS

INTRODUCTION

Making your own clothes is really rewarding. With so many terrific fabrics on sale, you can choose just what you like and end up with a garment that is totally you. And as well as making something that you won't find in the shops, you can also save money. What's not to like about that? But the question beginners always ask themselves is: where to start? This book is your perfect introduction. It shows you all you need to know to make a basic collection of clothes – three stylish skirts encompassing A-line, tailored and pleated designs, two must-have dresses with short- and long-sleeve variations, and a classic empire line dress.

In the book's first section you'll find clear pictures of all the kit a beginner sewer requires, followed by detailed instructions for the sewing techniques you need to make the garments to a professional standard. Next come the garments themselves, with photographs of how they'll look when they're finished, together with fabric suggestions for each. The clear step-by-step instructions that follow will take you right from cutting out your fabric to sewing on the last button. The final section of the book is the key to it all – the six garment patterns. Each of these has been drawn up in a range of sizes, so you'll also find full instructions for choosing the correct size for you as well as for scaling the patterns up and transferring them to paper.

So, all you need to do now is choose your fabric and start sewing. With this book by your side, you'll soon be part of the ever-growing army of home dressmakers. And who knows? You may even feel like making each pattern a few times in different fabrics to give a variety of different looks.

Happy sewing!

CUTTING OUT

Cutting out can make or break your project. But first you need to examine the fabric in the shop, looking for any flaws, such as a crooked pattern, and checking to see if the fabric has been cut properly from the roll – that is at a right angle to the selvedge. If it has not been cut properly, you will need to straighten the edge before cutting out. If the fabric is creased, press it; if washable, wash it to avoid shrinkage later. After this preparation, you will be ready to lay the pattern pieces on the fabric, pin in place, and cut out.

FABRIC GRAIN AND NAP

It is important that pattern pieces are cut on the correct grain; this will make the fabric hang correctly. The grain is the direction in which the yarns or threads that make up the fabric lie. The majority of pattern pieces need to be placed with the straight of grain symbol running parallel to the warp yarn. Some fabrics have a nap due to the pile, which means the fabric shadows when it is smoothed in one direction. A fabric with a one-way design or uneven stripes is also described as having a nap. Fabrics with nap are generally cut out with the nap running down, whereas those without nap can be cut out at any angle.

GRAIN ON WOVEN FABRICS

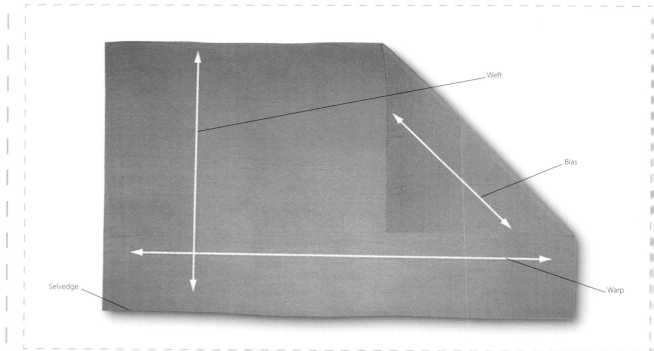

Weft

Bias

Selvedge

Warp

Yarns that run the length of the fabric are called warp yarns. They are stronger than weft yarns and less likely to stretch.

Weft yarns run crossways, over and under the warp yarns.

The bias grain is diagonal – running at 45 degrees to the warp and weft. A garment cut on the bias will follow the contours of the body.

The selvedge is the woven, non-frayable edge that runs parallel to the warp yarn.

PATTERN LAYOUT

For cutting out, fabric is usually folded selvedge to selvedge. With the fabric folded, the pattern is pinned on top, and both the right- and left-side pieces are cut out at the same time. If pattern pieces have to be cut from single layer fabric, remember to cut matching pairs. If a fabric has a design, lay the fabric design-side upwards so that you can arrange the pattern pieces to show off the design. If you have left- and right-side pattern pieces, they are cut on single fabric with the fabric right-side up and the pattern right-side up.

PINNING THE PATTERN TO THE FABRIC

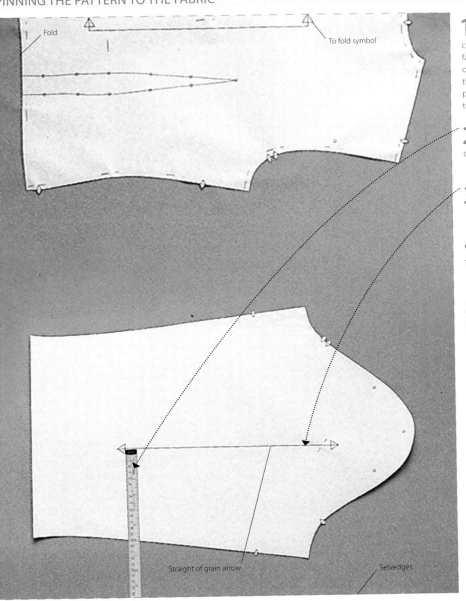

Fold

To fold symbol

Straight of grain arrow

Selvedges

1 The "to fold" symbol indicates the pattern piece is to be pinned carefully to the folded edge of the fabric. To check the straight of grain on the other pattern pieces, place the grain arrow so that it looks parallel to the selvedge, then pin to secure at one end of the arrow.

2 Measure from the pinned end to the selvedge and make a note of the measurement.

3 Measure from the other end of the arrow to the selvedge.

4 Move the pattern piece slightly until both measurements are the same, then pin in place.

5 Once the pattern is straight, pin around the rest of it, placing pins in the seam allowances.

CUTTING OUT ACCURATELY

Careful, smooth cutting around the pattern pieces will ensure that they join together accurately. Always cut out on a smooth, flat surface such as a table – the floor is not ideal – and be sure your scissors are sharp. Use the full blade of the scissors on long, straight edges, sliding the blades along the fabric; use smaller cuts around curves. Do not nibble or snip at the fabric.

HOW TO CUT

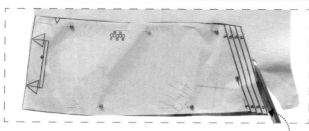

If you are right-handed, place your left hand on the pattern and fabric to hold them in place, and cut cleanly with the scissor blades at a right angle to the fabric.

MARKING NOTCHES

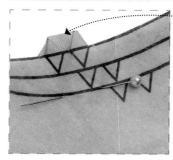

These symbols need to be marked on to the fabric as they are matching points. One of the easiest ways to do this is to cut out the mirror image of the notches in the fabric. Rather than cutting out double or triple notches separately, cut straight across from point to point.

MARKING DOTS

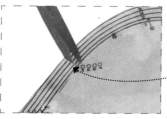

You can cut a small clip into the fabric to mark the dots that indicate the top of the shoulder on a sleeve. Alternatively, these can be marked with tailor's tacks (see opposite).

CLIPPING LINES

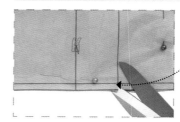

A small clip or snip into the fabric is a useful way to mark some of the lines that appear on a pattern, such as the centre front line and foldlines or notches and dart ends.

PATTERN MARKING

Once the pattern pieces have been cut out, but before you remove the pattern, you will need to mark the symbols shown on the pattern through to the fabric. There are various ways to do this. Tailor's tacks are good for circles and dots, or these can be marked with a water- or air-soluble pen. When using a pen, it's a good idea to test it on a piece of scrap fabric first. For lines, you can use trace tacks or a tracing wheel with dressmaker's carbon paper.

TRACE TACKS

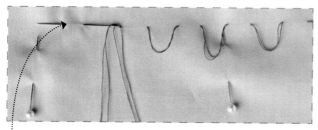

1 This is a really useful technique to mark centre front lines, foldlines, and placement lines. With double thread in your needle, stitch a row of loopy stitches, sewing along the line marked on the pattern.

2 Carefully pull away the tissue. Cut through the loops, then gently separate the layers of fabric to show the threads. Snip apart to leave thread tails in both of the fabric layers.

TAILOR'S TACKS

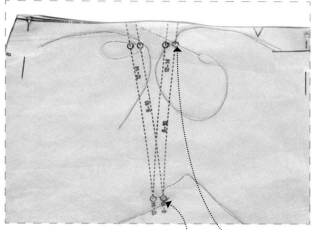

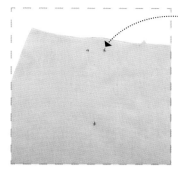

3 Carefully pull the pattern away. On the top side you will have four threads marking each dot. When you turn the fabric over, the dot positions will be marked with an X.

1 As there are often dots of different sizes on the pattern, choose a different colour thread for each dot size. It is then easy to match the colours as well as the dots. Have double thread in your needle, unknotted. Insert the needle through the dot from right to left, leaving a tail of thread. Be sure to go through the pattern and both layers of fabric.

2 Now stitch through the dot again, this time from top to bottom to make a loop. Cut through the loop, then snip off excess thread to leave a tail.

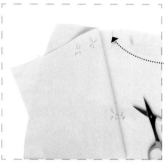

4 Gently turn back the two layers of fabric to separate them, then cut through the threads so that thread tails are left in both pieces of fabric.

TRACING PAPER AND WHEEL

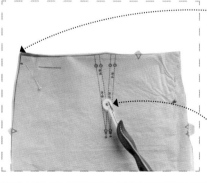

1 This method is not suitable for all fabrics as the marks may not be easy to remove. Slide dressmaker's carbon paper against the wrong side of the fabric.

2 Run a tracing wheel along the pattern lines (a ruler will help you make straight lines).

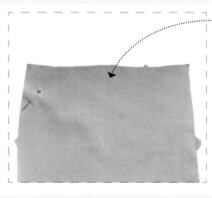

3 Remove the carbon paper and carefully pull off the pattern. There will be dotted lines marked on your fabric.

MARKER PENS

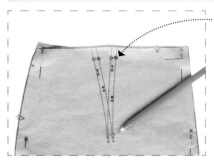

1 This method can only be used with a single layer of fabric. Press the point of the pen into the centre of the dot marked on the pattern.

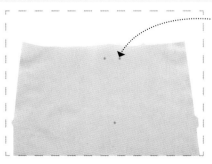

2 Carefully remove the pattern. The pen marks will have gone through the pattern on to the fabric. Be sure not to press the fabric before the pen marks are removed or they may become permanent.

HAND SEWING

Although sewing machines have eliminated the need for a lot of hand sewing, you still need to hand sew sometimes. The main hand sewing you will do is to hold fabric together temporarily before you do the permanent stitching, and for this you will use tacking stitches. The other important uses for hand sewing are to hold hems in place and to attach buttons, snaps, and hooks and eyes.

THREADING THE NEEDLE

When sewing by hand, cut your piece of thread to be no longer than the distance from your fingertips to your elbow. If the thread is much longer than this, it will knot as you sew.

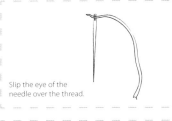

Slip the eye of the needle over the thread.

1 Hold your needle in your right hand and the end of the thread in your left. Keeping the thread still, place the eye of the needle over the thread.

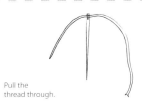

Pull the thread through.

2 If the needle will not slip over the thread, dampen your fingers and run the moisture across the eye of the needle. Pull the thread through.

Tie a knot at one end.

3 At the other end of the thread, tie a knot as shown or secure the thread as shown on the right.

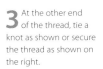

4 You are now ready to start your sewing.

SECURING THE THREAD

The ends of the thread must always be secured firmly. For temporary stitches such as tacking you can use a locking stitch, which is a stitch with a knot at the start and finish. For permanent stitches, a double stitch at the start and finish is the preferred choice.

DOUBLE STITCH

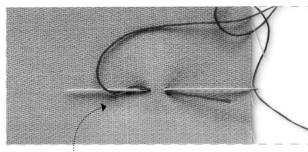

1 Take a stitch.

2 Go back through the stitch with the thread wrapped under the needle.

3 Pull through to make a knot.

BACK STITCH

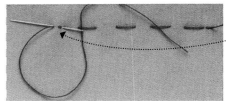

Make two small stitches in the same place.

LOCKING STITCH

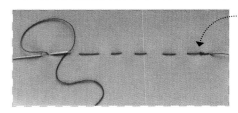

Start the stitching with a knot and finish by working a knot at the end.

TACKING STITCHES

Each of the many types of tacking stitches has its own individual use. Basic tacks hold two or more pieces of fabric together. Long and short tacks are an alternative version of the basic tacking stitch, often used when the tacking will stay in the work for some time.

BASIC TACKS

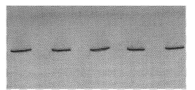

Starting with a knot and, using single thread, make straight stitches, evenly spaced.

LONG AND SHORT TACKS

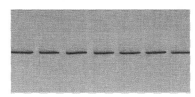

Make long stitches with a short space between each one.

HEM STITCHES

There are various hand stitches that can be used to hold a hem in place. Whichever of these you choose, ensure the stitches do not show on the right side.

FLAT FELL STITCH

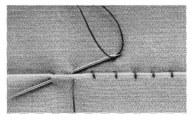

A strong, secure stitch to hold two layers permanently together. As well as being used for hems, this stitch is often used to secure bias bindings and linings. Work from right to left. Make a short, straight stitch at the edge of the fabric.

BLIND HEM STITCH

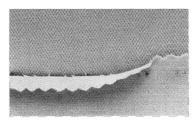

This stitch gives a very discreet finish to a hem. Working from right to left, fold the top edge of the fabric down and use a slip hem stitch (below left).

SLIP HEM STITCH

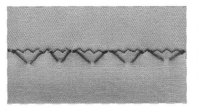

Also called a catch stitch, this is used primarily for securing hems. It looks similar to herringbone (right). Work from right to left. Take a short horizontal stitch into one layer and then the other.

HERRINGBONE STITCH

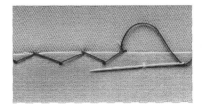

A very useful stitch as it is secure yet has some movement in it. It is used to secure hems and interlinings. Work from left to right. Take a small horizontal stitch into one layer and then the other, so the thread crosses itself.

ATTACHING HOOKS AND EYES

There is a multitude of different types of hook and eye fasteners available to buy. They are made from metal and can either be silver or black in colour. Choose the colour that best suits your garment.

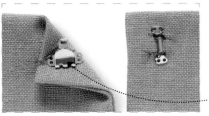

1 A hook and eye fastener for waistbands is large and flat. Tack both the hook and eye in position. Do not tack through their securing holes.

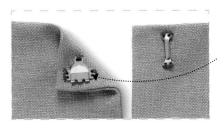

2 Buttonhole stitch through all the securing holes on both hook and eye.

MACHINE SEWING

When making a garment, fabric is joined together using seams. The most common seam is a plain seam, which is suitable for a wide variety of fabrics and garments.

SECURING THE THREAD

The ends of the thread must always be secured firmly. For temporary stitches such as tacking you can use a locking stitch, which is a stitch with a knot at the start and finish. For permanent stitches, a double stitch at the start and finish is the preferred choice.

TIE THE ENDS

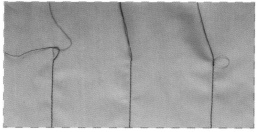

1 Pull on the top thread and it will pull up a loop – this is the bobbin thread.

2 Pull the loop through to the top.

3 Tie the two threads together and trim.

REVERSE STITCH

1 When starting to machine, stitch a couple of stitches forward, then hold in the reverse button and reverse over them. Continue forward again.

2 At the end of the seam, reverse again to secure the stitches.

LOCKING STITCH

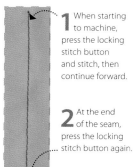

1 When starting to machine, press the locking stitch button and stitch, then continue forward.

2 At the end of the seam, press the locking stitch button again.

PLAIN SEAM

A plain seam is 1.5cm (⁵⁄₈in) wide. It is important that the seam is stitched accurately at this measurement, otherwise the garment will end up being the wrong size and shape. There are guides on the plate of the sewing machine to help align the fabric correctly.

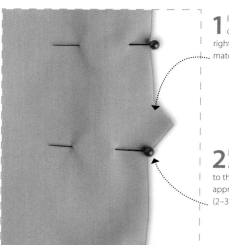

1 Pin the two pieces of fabric together, right side to right side, matching notches.

2 Place the pins at right angles to the raw edge at approximately 5–8cm (2–3in) intervals.

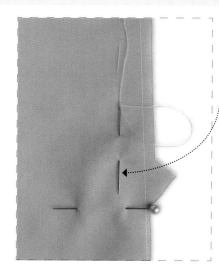

3 Tack the two pieces of fabric together about 1cm (³⁄₈in) from the raw edge, removing each individual pin as you reach it.

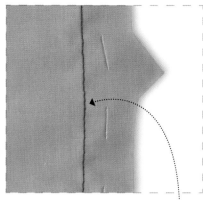

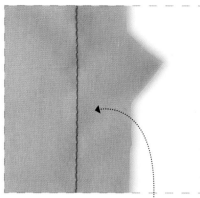

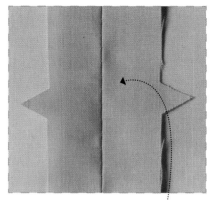

4 Machine the seam at 1.5cm (⅝in), securing it at either end by your chosen technique.

5 Carefully remove the tacking stitches.

6 Press the seam open on the wrong side.

SEAM NEATENING

It is important that the raw edges of the seam are neatened or finished – this will make the seam hard-wearing and prevent fraying. The method of neatening will depend on the style of garment that is being made and the fabric you are using.

PINKED

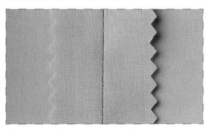

This method of neatening is ideal for fabrics that do not fray badly. Using pinking shears, trim as little as possible off the raw edge.

ZIGZAGGED

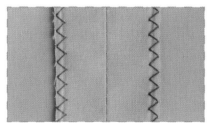

All sewing machines will make a zigzag stitch. It is an ideal stitch for stopping the edges fraying and is suitable for all types of fabric. Stitch in from the raw edge, then trim back to the zigzag stitch. Use a stitch width of 2.0 and a stitch length of 1.5.

3-THREAD OVERLOCK STITCH

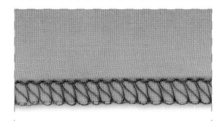

This is made using an overlocker (see pp.16–17), which wraps the thread around the edge to give a secure and professional finish that will stop the fabric from fraying.

DECORATIVE STITCHING

Most of your machine sewing will consist of sewing seams and neatening them so your machine stitching will not be visible on your finished work. Sometimes though, you will add a touch of decorative stitching that is designed to be on show. This can be sewn using a matching or a contrasting colour thread.

TOP-STITCHING

This is worked using a straight stitch and is used to give a decorative, sharp edge to necklines, armholes, collars, and pockets. Use a stitch length of 3.0 or 3.5 and machine on the right side of the work. Use the edge of the machine foot as a guide to help you achieve a straight line.

DARTS

A dart is used to give shape to a piece of fabric so that it can fit around the contours of the body. Some darts are stitched following straight stitching lines and other darts are stitched following a slightly curved line. Always stitch a dart from the point to the wide end as then you will be able to sink the machine needle into the point accurately and securely.

PLAIN DART

This is the most common type of dart and is used to give shaping to the bust in the bodice. It is also found at the waist in skirts and trousers to give shape from the waist to the hip.

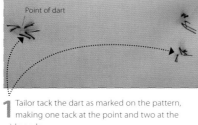

Point of dart

1 Tailor tack the dart as marked on the pattern, making one tack at the point and two at the wide ends.

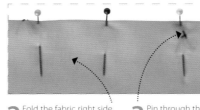

2 Fold the fabric right side to right side, matching the tailor's tacks.

3 Pin through the tailor's tacks to match them.

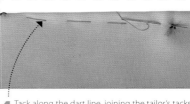

4 Tack along the dart line, joining the tailor's tacks. Remove the pins.

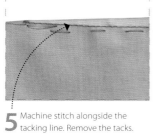

5 Machine stitch alongside the tacking line. Remove the tacks.

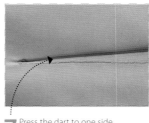

6 Sew the machine threads back into the stitching line of the dart to secure them.

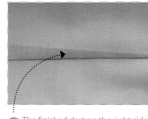

7 Press the dart to one side.

8 The finished dart on the right side.

SHAPING DARTS TO FIT

Our bodies have curves, and the straight line of the dart may not sit closely enough to our own personal shape. The dart can be stitched slightly concave or convex so it follows our contours. Do not curve the dart by more than 3mm (⅛in) from the straight line.

CONVEX DART

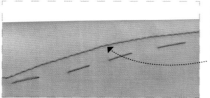

Use this for fuller shapes. Stitch the dart slightly inside the normal stitching line, to make a smooth convex curve.

CONCAVE DART

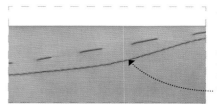

This is for thinner bodies as it takes up more fabric. Stitch the dart slightly outside the normal stitching line, in a smooth concave curve.

CONTOUR OR DOUBLE-POINTED DART

This type of dart is like two darts joined together at their wide ends. It is used to give shape at the waist of a dress. It will contour the fabric from the bust into the waist and then from the waist out towards the hip.

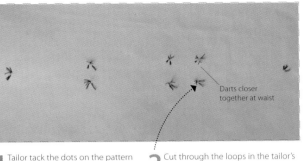

Darts closer together at waist

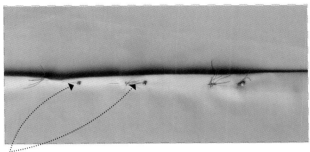

1 Tailor tack the dots on the pattern that mark the dart.

2 Cut through the loops in the tailor's tacks and remove the pattern.

3 Bring the tailor's tacks together, keeping the fabric right side to right side, and pin the tacks together.

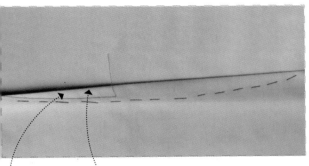

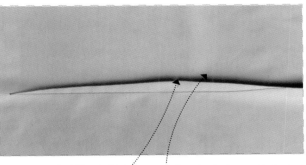

4 Make a row of tacking stitches just outside the pin line.

5 Machine stitch following the tailor-tack line, starting at one end and curving out to the widest point, then in to the other end. Secure the machine stitching at both ends.

6 Remove the tacking.

7 Clip across the fold in the fabric at the widest point, to allow the dart to be pressed to one side.

8 Press the dart to one side. Contour darts are normally pressed towards the centre front or centre back.

PRESSING A DART

If a dart is pressed incorrectly it can spoil the look of a garment. For successful pressing you will need a tailor's ham and a steam iron on a steam setting. A pressing cloth may be required for delicate fabrics such as silk, satin, and chiffon, and for lining fabrics.

1 Place the fabric, right side down, on the tailor's ham. The point of the dart should be over the end of the ham.

2 Press the fabric around the point of the dart.

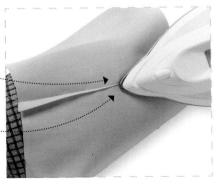

3 Move the iron from the point towards the wide end of the dart to press the dart flat, open, or to one side, depending on the type of dart.

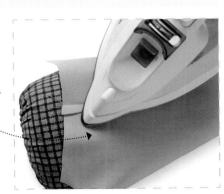

INTERFACINGS

An interfacing may be non-fusible (sew-in) or fusible and is only attached to certain parts of a garment. Parts that are normally interfaced include the collar and cuffs and the facings.

NON-FUSIBLE INTERFACINGS

All of these interfacings need to be tacked to the main fabric around the edges prior to construction of the work or seam neatening.

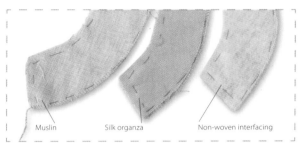

Muslin   Silk organza   Non-woven interfacing

FUSIBLE INTERFACINGS

A fusible interfacing is used in the same areas as a sew-in interfacing. To prevent the fusible interfacing from showing on the right side of the work, use pinking shears on the edge of the interfacing.

Lightweight woven fusible interfacing

Knitted fusible interfacing

Non-woven fusible interfacing

HOW TO APPLY A NON-FUSIBLE INTERFACING

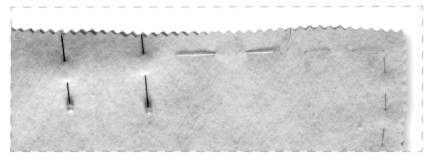

1 Place the interfacing on to the wrong side of the fabric, aligning the cut edges.

2 Pin in place.

3 Using a basic tacking stitch, tack the interfacing to the fabric or facing at 1cm (³/₈in) within the seam allowance.

HOW TO APPLY A FUSIBLE INTERFACING

1 Place the fabric on the pressing surface, wrong side up, making sure it is straight and not wrinkled.

2 Place the sticky side (this feels gritty) of the chosen interfacing on the fabric.

3 Cover with a dry pressing cloth and spray the cloth with a fine mist of water.

4 Place a steam iron, on a steam setting, on top of the pressing cloth.

5 Leave the iron in place for at least 10 seconds before moving it to the next area of fabric.

6 Check to see if the interfacing is fused to the fabric by rolling the fabric. If the interfacing is still loose in places, repeat the pressing process.

7 When the fabric has cooled down, the fusing process will be complete. Then pin the pattern back on to the fabric and transfer the pattern markings as required.

FACINGS

The simplest way to finish the neck or armhole of a garment is to apply a facing. The neckline can be any shape to have a facing applied, from a curve to a square to a V, and many more. Some facings and necklines can add interest to the centre back or centre front of a garment.

APPLYING INTERFACING TO A FACING

All facings require interfacing. The interfacing is to give structure to the facing and to hold it in shape. A fusible interfacing is the best choice and should be cut on the same grain as the facing. Choose an interfacing that is lighter in weight than the main fabric.

INTERFACING FOR HEAVY FABRIC

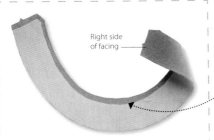

Right side of facing

For a heavy-weight fabric use a medium-weight fusible interfacing. Remove the seam allowance on the interfacing on the inner curve to reduce bulk.

INTERFACING FOR LIGHT FABRIC

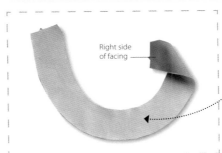

Right side of facing

For a light- to medium-weight fabric, choose a lightweight interfacing and fuse it over the complete facing.

CONSTRUCTION OF A FACING

The facing may be in two or three pieces in order to fit around a neck or armhole edge. The facing sections need to be joined together prior to being attached. The photographs here show an interfaced neck facing in three pieces.

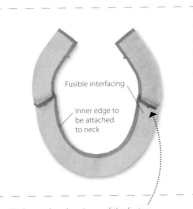

Fusible interfacing

Inner edge to be attached to neck

1 Tack together the pieces of the facing at the shoulder seams.

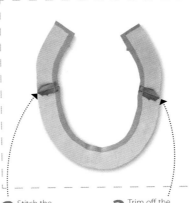

2 Stitch the shoulder seams and press open.

3 Trim off the outer corners on the shoulder seams.

4 The right side of the facing, ready to attach to the neckline.

HEMLINES

The lower edge of a garment is normally finished with a hem. Sometimes the style of the garment dictates the type of hem used, and sometimes the fabric.

MARKING A HEMLINE

On a garment such as a skirt or a dress it is important that the hemline is level all around. Even if the fabric has been cut straight, some styles of skirt – such as A-line or circular – will "drop", which means that the hem edge is longer in some places. This is due to the fabric stretching where it is not on the straight of the grain. Hang the garment for 24 hours in a warm room before hemming so you do not end up with an uneven hem.

USING A RULER

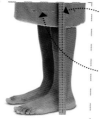

1 Put on the skirt or dress but no shoes. With the end of the ruler on the floor, have a helper measure and mark.

2 Use pins to mark the crease line of the proposed hem. Ensure the measurement from floor to pin line is the same all the way round.

USING A DRESSMAKER'S DUMMY

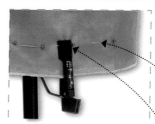

1 Adjust the dummy to your height and measurements. Place the skirt or dress on the dummy.

2 The hem marker on its stand will hold the fabric. Use the marker to mark the crease line of the proposed hem.

3 Slide a pin through the slot in the marker, then gently release the marker.

HAND-STITCHED HEMS

One of the most popular ways to secure a hem edge is by hand. Hand stitching is discreet and, if a fine hand-sewing needle is used, the stitching should not show on the right side of the work. Always finish the raw edge before stitching the hem.

TIPS FOR SEWING HEMS BY HAND

1 Always use a single thread in the needle – a polyester all-purpose thread is ideal for hemming.
2 Once the raw edge of the hem allowance has been neatened (see below), secure it using a hem stitch (see p.11). Take half of the stitch into the neatened edge and the other half into the wrong side of the garment fabric.

3 Start and finish the hand stitching with a double stitch, not a knot, because knots will catch and pull the hem down.
4 It is a good idea to take a small back stitch every 10cm (4in) or so to make sure that if the hem does come loose in one place it will not all unravel.

OVERLOCKED FINISH

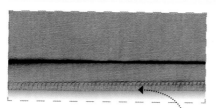

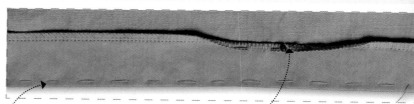

1 Using a 3-thread overlock stitch, stitch along the raw edge of the hem allowance.

2 Gently press the hem up into position and tack close to the crease.

3 Roll back the overlocked edge and stitch the hem in place.

4 Press carefully to prevent the overlocking from being imprinted on the right side.

CURVED HEM FINISH

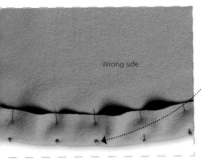

1 Fold up the hemline and pin, placing the pins vertically to avoid squashing the fullness out of the raw upper edge.

Wrong side

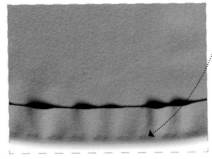

2 Tack the hem into position close to the crease line. Remove the pins.

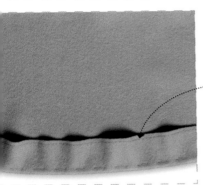

3 Make a row of long machine stitches, length 5.0, close to the raw upper edge of the turned-up hem.

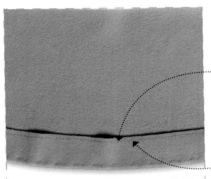

4 Pull on one of the threads of the long stitches to tighten the fabric and ease out the fullness.

5 Use the steam iron to shrink out the remainder of the fullness. The hem is now ready to be stitched in place by hand or machine.

MACHINED HEMS

On some occasions, the hem or edge of a garment or other item is turned up and secured using the sewing machine. It can be stitched with a straight stitch, a zigzag stitch, or a blind hem stitch if you have the appropriate machine foot. Hems can also be made on the overlocker (see p.16).

DOUBLE-TURN HEM

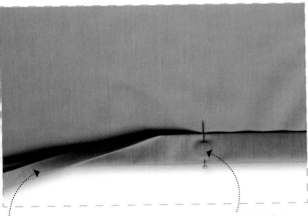

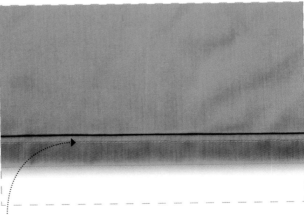

1 This hem will add weight at the edge. Fold up the raw edge of the fabric once and then fold again.

2 Pin in place, then press.

3 Machine using a straight stitch, close to the upper fold.

SLEEVES

Sleeves come in all shapes and lengths, and form an important part of the design of a garment. A set-in sleeve should always hang from the end of the wearer's shoulder, without wrinkles. The lower end of the sleeve may be finished by means of a cuff.

INSERTING A SET-IN SLEEVE

A set-in sleeve should feature a smooth sleeve head that fits on the end of your shoulder accurately. This is achieved by the use of ease stitches, which are long stitches used to tighten the fabric but not gather it.

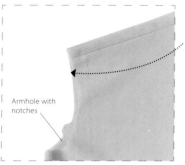

1 Machine the side seams and the shoulder seams on the garment and press them open.

Armhole with notches

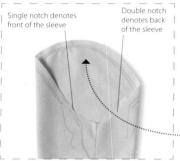

Single notch denotes front of the sleeve

Double notch denotes back of the sleeve

2 Machine the sleeve seam and press open. Turn the sleeve to the right side.

3 Around the sleeve head, machine two rows of long stitches between the notches – one row at 1cm (³∕₈in) from the edge and the second row at 1.2cm (¹∕₂in). These are the ease stitches.

4 Place the sleeve into the armhole, right side to right side. Match the underarm seams and the notches.

5 Match the highest point of the sleeve to the shoulder.

6 Pull up the ease stitches until the sleeve fits neatly in the armhole.

7 Pin from the sleeve side.

8 Machine the sleeve in place, starting at the underarm seam and using a 1.5cm (⁵∕₈in) seam allowance. When you machine, have the sleeve on top and keep the machining straight over the shoulder.

9 Overlap the machining at the underarm to reinforce the stitching.

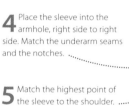

10 Stitch around the sleeve again, inside the seam allowance.

11 Trim the raw edges of the sleeve.

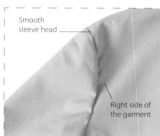

Smooth sleeve head

Right side of the garment

12 Neaten the seam with a zigzag or overlock stitch, then turn the sleeve through the armhole. Do not press or you will flatten the sleeve head.

SLEEVE HEMS

The simplest way to finish a sleeve is with a self hem. Here the edge of the sleeve is turned up onto itself. Alternative finishes include inserting elastic into a casing or attaching a cuff.

SELF HEM

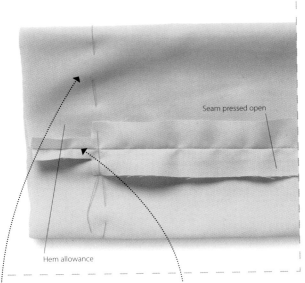

Seam pressed open

Hem allowance

1 Mark the final length of the sleeve with a row of tacking stitches.

2 Remove the excess seam allowance in the hem area.

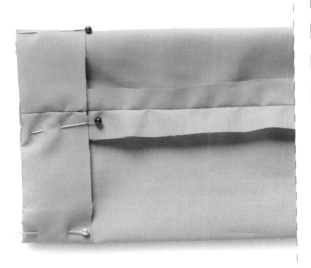

3 Turn up the hem along the tacked line.

4 Match the seams. Pin in place.

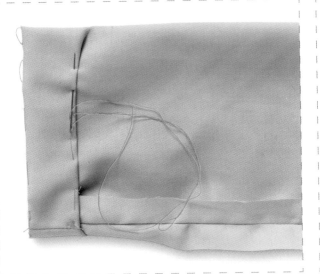

5 Turn under the top edge of the hem allowance by 1cm (³/₈in) and pin.

6 Tack to secure.

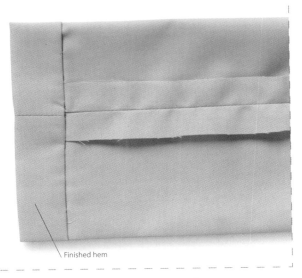

Finished hem

7 Hand stitch the sleeve hem in place using a slip stitch.

REDUCING SEAM BULK

Seams should lie flat and not be bulky on the right side. To make sure of this, any excess fabric must be removed from the seam allowances. One technique for doing this is known as layering. On curved seams you may also have to cut out notches or clip through the seam allowance, depending on whether the curve is an inner or an outer curve.

LAYERING A SEAM

On the majority of fabrics, if the seam is on the edge of the work, the amount of fabric in the seam needs reducing. Leave the seam allowance that lies closest to the outside of the garment full width, but reduce the seam allowance that lies closest to the body.

Cut along one side of the seam allowance to reduce the fabric in the seam allowance by half to one-third of its original width.

REDUCING SEAM BULK ON AN INNER CURVE

For an inner curve to lie flat, the seam must be layered and notched, then understitched to hold the facing in place and stop it from rolling to the right side.

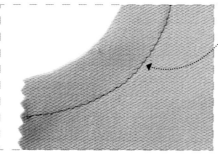

1 Stitch the seam on the inner curve to attach the facing.

2 Layer the seam allowance (see above), then cut out V notches to reduce the bulk.

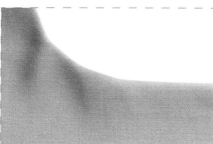

3 Turn to the right side and press.

facing

4 Open out the seam and understitch by machining the seam allowances to the facing.

REDUCING SEAM BULK ON AN OUTER CURVE

An outer curve also needs layering but in this case the seam allowance is clipped so the seam will lie flat. After turning to the right side and pressing, the seam is understitched.

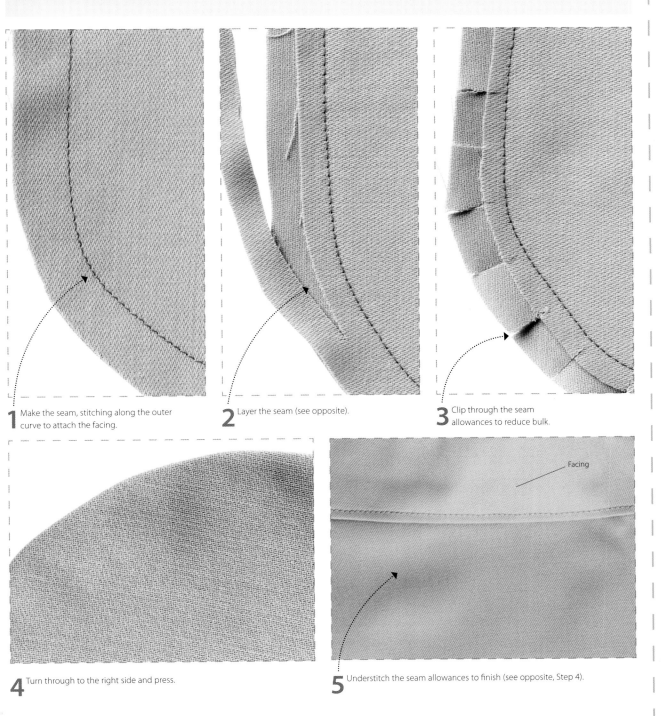

1 Make the seam, stitching along the outer curve to attach the facing.

2 Layer the seam (see opposite).

3 Clip through the seam allowances to reduce bulk.

4 Turn through to the right side and press.

Facing

5 Understitch the seam allowances to finish (see opposite, Step 4).

ZIPS

The zip is probably the most used of all fastenings. There are a great many types available, in a variety of lengths, colours, and materials, but they all fall into one of five categories: skirt or trouser zips, metal or jeans zips, concealed zips, open-ended zips, and decorative zips.

LAPPED ZIP

A lapped zip features one side of the seam – the left-hand side – lapping over the teeth of the zip to conceal them. You will need to use a zip foot on your machine.

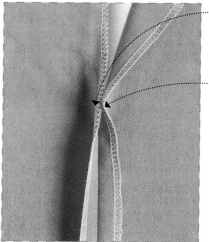

1 Stitch the seam, leaving enough of it open to accommodate the zip.

2 Secure the end of the stitching.

3 Insert the right-hand side of the zip first. Fold back the right-hand seam allowance by 1.2cm (¹/₂in). This folded edge will not be in line with the seam.

4 Place the folded edge against the zip teeth. Tack.

5 Using the zip foot, stitch along the tack line to secure the zip tape to the fabric. Stitch from the bottom of the zip to the top.

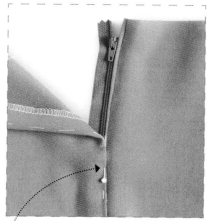

6 Fold back the left-hand seam allowance by 1.5cm (⁵/₈in). Place the folded edge over the machine line of the other side. Pin and then tack.

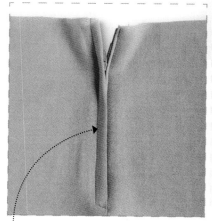

7 Starting at the bottom of the zip, stitch across from the centre seamline and then up the left side of the zip. The finished zip should have its teeth covered by the fabric.

CONCEALED OR INVISIBLE ZIP

With this type of zip the teeth are on the reverse and nothing except the pull is seen on the front. The zip is inserted before the seam is stitched. A special concealed zip foot is required for stitching this zip in position.

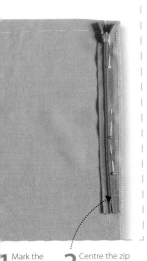

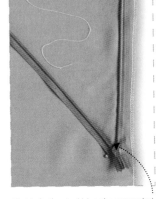

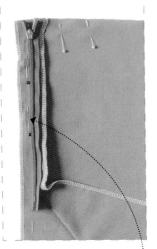

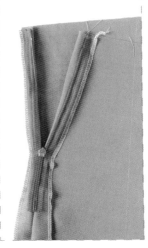

1 Mark the seam allowance with tacking stitches.

2 Centre the zip over the tack line, right side of zip to right side of fabric. Pin in place down one side.

3 Undo the zip. Using the concealed zip foot, stitch under the teeth from the top of the zip. Stop when the foot hits the zip pull and do two reverse stitches.

4 Do the zip up. Place the other side of the fabric to the zip. Match along the upper edge. Pin the other side of the zip tape in place.

5 Open the zip again. Using the concealed zip foot, stitch down the other side of the zip to attach to the other side of the fabric. Remove any tacking stitches.

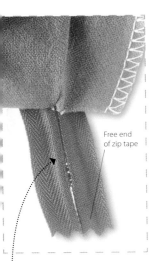

Free end of zip tape

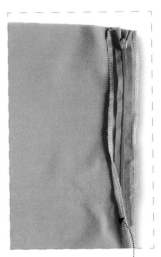

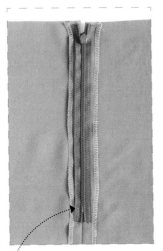

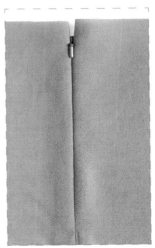

6 Close the zip. On the wrong side at the bottom of the zip, the two rows of stitching that hold in the zip should finish at the same place.

7 Stitch the seam below the zip using the normal machine foot. There will be a small gap of about 3mm (⅛in) between the stitching line for the zip and that for the seam.

8 Stitch the last 3cm (1¼in) of the zip tape to just the seam allowances. This will stop the zip pulling loose.

9 On the right side, the zip is completely concealed, with only the pull visible at the top.

BUTTONS

Buttons are one of the oldest forms of fastening. They come in many shapes and sizes, and can be made from a variety of materials including shell, bone, plastic, nylon, and metal. Buttons are normally sewn on by hand, although a two-hole button can be sewn on by machine.

SEWING ON A TWO-HOLE BUTTON

This is the most popular type of button and requires a thread shank to be made when sewing in place. A cocktail stick on top of the button will help you to make the shank.

1 Position the button on the fabric. Start with a double stitch and double thread in the needle.

2 Place a cocktail stick on top of the button. Stitch up and down through the holes, going over the stick.

3 Remove the cocktail stick.

4 Wrap the thread around the thread loops under the button to make a shank.

5 Take the thread through to the back of the fabric.

6 Buttonhole stitch over the loop of threads on the back of the work.

SEWING ON A FOUR-HOLE BUTTON

This is stitched in the same way as a two-hole button except that the threads make an X over the top of the button.

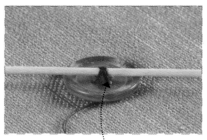

1 Position the button on the fabric. Place a cocktail stick on the button.

2 Using double thread, stitch diagonally between the holes of the button to make an X on top of the cocktail stick.

3 Remove the cocktail stick.

4 Wrap the thread around the thread loops under the button to make the shank.

5 On the reverse of the fabric, buttonhole stitch over the X-shaped thread loops.

BUTTONHOLES

VERTICAL OR HORIZONTAL?

Generally, buttonholes are only placed vertically on a garment with a placket or strip to contain the buttonholes. All other buttonholes should be horizontal. Any strain on the buttonhole will then be taken by the end stop and prevent the button from coming undone.

HORIZONTAL BUTTONHOLES

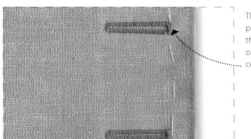

These are positioned with the end stop on the tacked centre line.

VERTICAL BUTTONHOLES

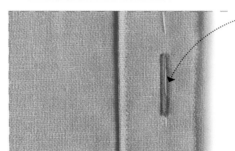

These are positioned with the buttonhole centred on the tacked centre line.

STAGES OF A BUTTONHOLE

A sewing machine stitches a buttonhole in three stages. The stitch can be varied slightly in width and length to suit the fabric, but the stitches need to be tight and close together.

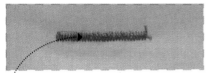

1 Machine the first side of the buttonhole.

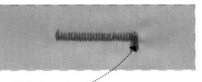

2 Stitch a bar tack at one end.

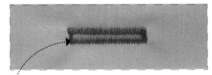

3 Machine the second side and bar tack at the other end.

MACHINE-MADE BUTTONHOLES

Modern sewing machines can stitch various types of buttonhole, suitable for all kinds of garments. On many machines the button fits into a special foot, and a sensor on the machine determines the correct size of buttonhole. The width and length of the stitch can be altered to suit the fabric. Once the buttonhole has been stitched, always use a buttonhole chisel (see p.13) to slash through. This ensures that the cut is clean.

BASIC BUTTONHOLE

The most popular shape for a buttonhole is square on both ends.

ROUND-END BUTTONHOLE

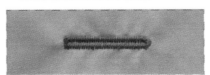

A buttonhole featuring one rounded end and one square end is used on lightweight jackets.

KEYHOLE BUTTONHOLE

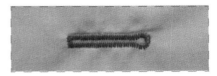

This is also called a tailor's buttonhole. It has a square end and a keyhole end, and is used on jackets and coats.

CLASSIC A-LINE SKIRT

This A-line skirt will never go out of fashion and can be worn at all times of the year and to all occasions. It is also one of the easiest garments for a beginner to make. It has only three pattern pieces – a front, a back, and a waistband. The skirt needs to fit comfortably around the waist and across the tummy, so check your measurements carefully against the pattern.

BEFORE YOU START

YOU WILL NEED

- 1.3m (51in) x 150cm (59in) fabric
- 1 x reel matching all-purpose sewing thread
- 1 x reel contrasting all-purpose sewing thread for pattern marking
- 1m x waistband interfacing
- 1 x 22cm (8¹/₂in) skirt zip
- 1 x button

PREPARING THE PATTERN

- This skirt is made using Skirt Pattern One (see pp.50-51)
- Follow the instructions (see pp.48–49) to copy or download the pattern in your size

GARMENT CONSTRUCTION

This A-line skirt is shaped by the two darts in the front and back. There is a zip in the left-hand side. The narrow waistband is fastened with a button and buttonhole fastening. The finished skirt should sit just above the knee.

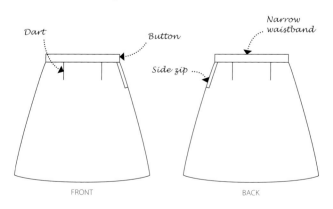

Dart   Button   Side zip   Narrow waistband

FRONT   BACK

HOW TO MAKE THE CLASSIC A-LINE SKIRT

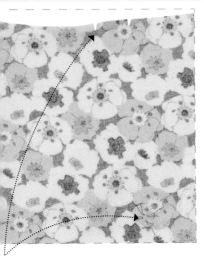

1 Cut out the fabric and mark the start of the darts with tailor's tacks (see p.14). **Clip the end of the darts** on the raw edge (see p.8).

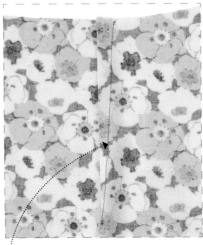

2 Make the darts (see p.14) and press towards the centre of the garment.

3 Neaten the side seams on the back and the front using a 3-thread overlock stitch or a small zigzag stitch (see pp.12–13).

4 Stitch the LH (left hand) side seam, leaving a gap for the zip. Press the seam open then insert a zip (see p.24).

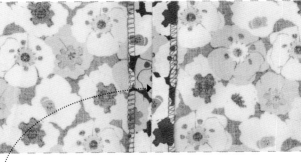

5 Stitch the RH (right hand) side seam and press the seam open (see pp.12–13).

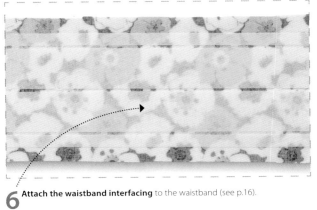

6 Attach the waistband interfacing to the waistband (see p.16).

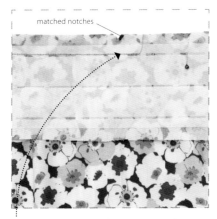

matched notches

7 **Attach the waistband** to the skirt, matching the notches.

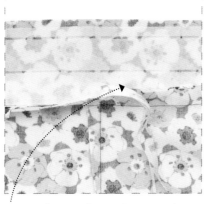

8 **Layer the seam allowance** by trimming the waistband side of the seam to half its width (see p.22). Press towards the waistband.

9 **Fold the waistband** RS (right side) to RS. Pin then **stitch the ends of the waistband**.

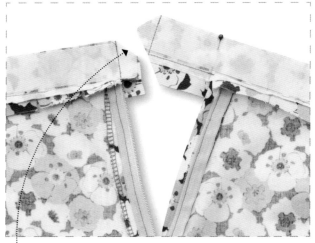

10 **Clip the ends of the waistband** to reduce bulk.

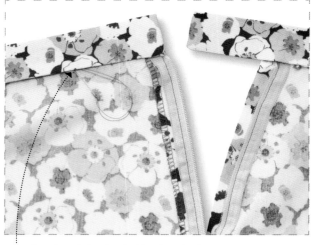

11 **Turn the waistband** to the RS, pushing the clipped ends out. Fold under the raw edge, then pin and **handstitch in place**.

12 **Neaten the hem edge** by overlocking (see p.18). Turn up a 4cm (1½in) hem and **handstitch in place**.

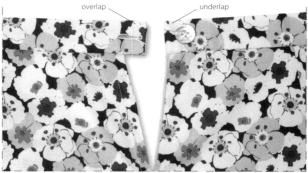

overlap   underlap

13 **Make a buttonhole** on the overlap of the waistband (see p.27). **Sew a button** on the underlap (see p.26).

Skirt Pattern Two

CLASSIC TAILORED SKIRT

A straight skirt is a staple garment in every woman's wardrobe. It could be the bottom half of a suit, made in a party fabric for a night out, or just be a simple, hardworking everyday skirt. The vent in the centre back hemline ensures you won't have trouble walking whatever the occasion. The skirt should be close-fitting, so choose the pattern size by your hip measurement.

BEFORE YOU START

YOU WILL NEED

- 1m (39¼in) x 150cm (59in) fabric
- 1 x reel matching all-purpose sewing thread
- 1 x reel contrasting all-purpose sewing thread for pattern marking
- 50cm (19½in) lightweight fusible interfacing
- 1 x 18cm (7in) skirt zip

PREPARING THE PATTERN

- This skirt is made using Skirt Pattern Two (see pp.52–53)
- Follow the instructions (see pp.48–49) to copy or download the pattern in your size

GARMENT CONSTRUCTION

This close-fitting skirt narrows slightly towards the hem and has a centre back vent. One dart in the front and two in the back shape the skirt to the waist and there is a zip in the centre back. The waistline is finished with a facing.

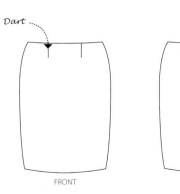

FRONT   BACK

HOW TO MAKE THE CLASSIC TAILORED SKIRT

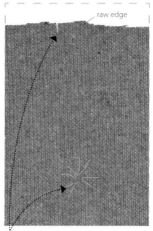

raw edge

1 **Cut out the fabric and mark the darts** using tailor's tacks (see p.14). **Clip the end of the darts** on the raw edge (see p.8).

2 **Make the darts** (see p.14) and press towards the centre of the garment.

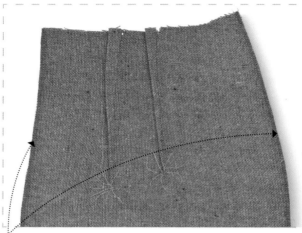

3 **Neaten the side and CB (centre back) seams** using a 3-thread overlock stitch or a small zigzag stitch (see p.13).

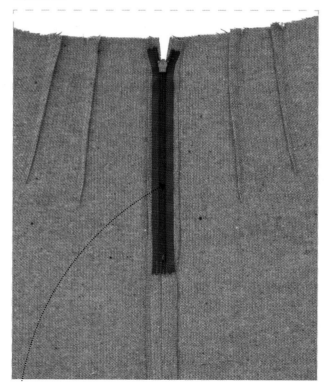

4 **Insert a concealed zip** at the CB (see p.25).

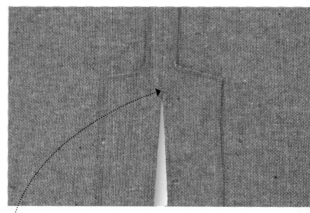

5 **Stitch the remainder of the CB seam,** stopping at the dot marking the top of the vent. Press the seam open.

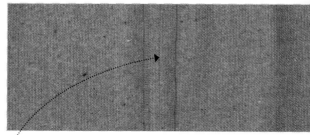

6 **Join the front to the back** at the side seams and press the seams open.

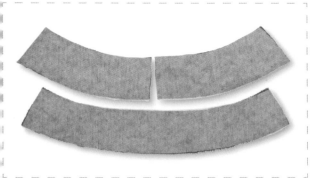

7 **Attach a lightweight fusible interfacing** to the waist facing pieces (see p.16).

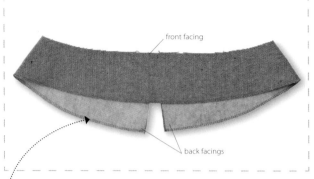

8 **Join the front and back facings** and press the seams open. Neaten the lower edge of the facing using a 3-thread overlock stitch or a small zigzag stitch.

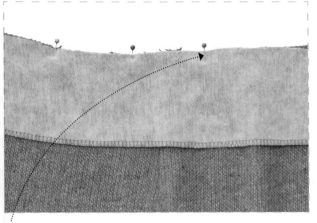

9 **Place the facing to the skirt** at the waist edge RS (right side) to RS, matching the side seams and matching at the top of the zip. Pin and machine.

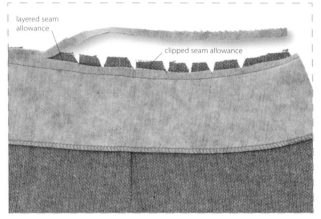

10 **Layer the seam allowance** by trimming the facing side of the seam to half its width. **Clip the seam allowance** to reduce bulk (see p.22).

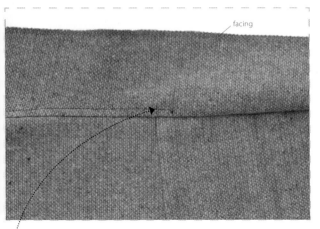

11 **Press the seam** towards the facing and **understitch** (see p.23).

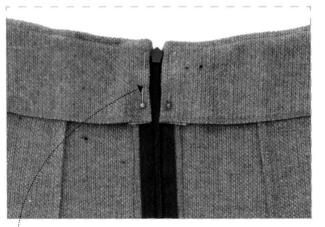

12 **Turn the facing** to the inside then, at the CB, fold the edge of the facing in to meet the zip tape. Pin and **handstitch in place**.

13 **At the vent,** snip through the seam allowance on the LH (left hand) side and press the seam extension to the RH (right hand) side.

14 **Machine the extension in place.**

15 From the RS, the top of the vent can be seen as a line of stitching.

16 **Neaten the hem edge** (see pp.18–19). On each side of the vent, **remove the surplus fabric** in the hem allowance.

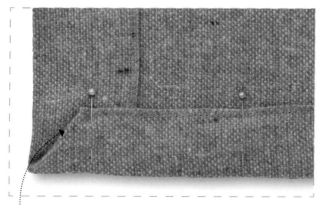

17 **Mitre the hem** at the bottom of the vent. Pin.

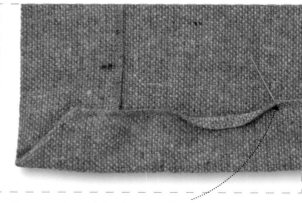

18 **Turn up the remainder of the hem,** pin and handstitch in place.

Skirt Pattern Three

CLASSIC PLEATED SKIRT

In this skirt you'll be introduced to making box pleats and adding a yoke. You should take care and work accurately as you'll have to transfer all the marks for the folds from the pattern to your fabric. The flattering yoke over the tummy avoids any bulk. Choose your size by your hip measurement to make sure the pleats hang straight and be sure you know the width of your belt before you construct the carriers. Once you've finished, you'll have a timeless pleated skirt to add to your wardrobe.

BEFORE YOU START

YOU WILL NEED

- 1.5m (59in) x 150cm (59in) fabric
- 2 x reels matching all-purpose polyester sewing thread
- 2 x reels contrasting all-purpose sewing thread in two different colours for pattern marking
- 1 x 18cm (7in) skirt zip
- 50cm (20in) medium-weight interfacing
- 50cm (20in) lightweight interfacing

PREPARING THE PATTERN

- This skirt is made using Skirt Pattern Three (see pp.54–55)
- Follow the instructions (see pp.49–49) to copy or download the pattern in your size

GARMENT CONSTRUCTION

This classic pleated unlined skirt has three box pleats at the back and front. The skirt has a self-lined yoke that sits just below the natural waistline, with two belt carriers at the front and back. There is a zip in the left-hand side.

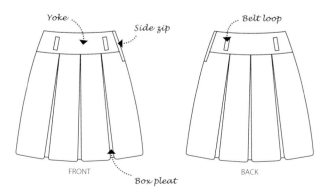

Yoke · · · Side zip · · · Belt loop

FRONT · · · Box pleat   BACK

HOW TO MAKE THE CLASSIC PLEATED SKIRT

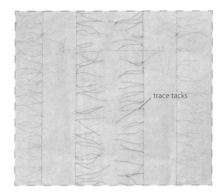

trace tacks

1 **Cut out the fabric** and mark the fold lines and crease lines with trace tacks (see p.8), each type of line in a different coloured thread. Cut through the loops in the trace tacks.

2 **Remove the pattern** carefully so as not to pull the trace tacks out.

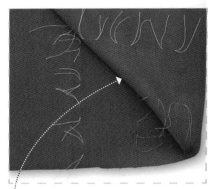

3 **Fold the fabric** RS (right side) to RS and match tacks of the same colour to each other. Pin along the line of tacks that is farther from the fold. Tack through the pins then remove the pins.

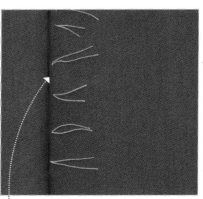

4 From the RS, the tacked pleat can be seen with its trace tacks.

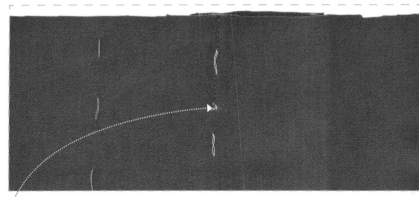

5 On the WS (wrong side), **machine along this tack line** to the dot marking on the pattern.

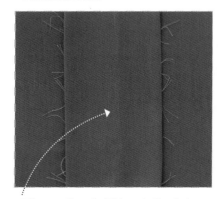

6 **Press gently** on the WS **to make the pleat**. Repeat for each pleat. For sharp pleats, press more heavily placing a pressing cloth over the fabric.

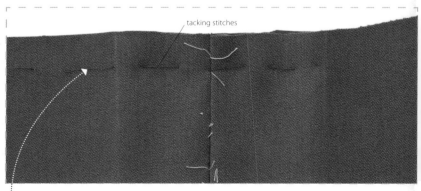

tacking stitches

7 On the RS (right side), **tack around the waist** to hold the pleats in place.

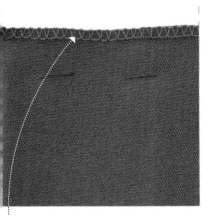

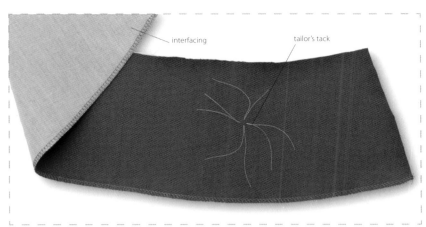

interfacing   tailor's tack

8 **Neaten the waist edge,** including the top edge of the pleats, using a 3-thread overlock stitch or a small zigzag stitch (see p.13).

9 **Attach a medium-weight fusible interfacing** to one front and one back yoke (see p.16), join the yoke pieces together at the RH (right hand) side, press the seams open, and neaten the lower edge using a 3-thread overlock stitch or a small zigzag stitch. **Mark the position of the belt carriers** with tailor's tacks (see p.9).

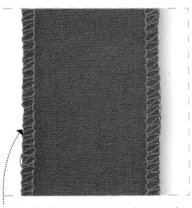

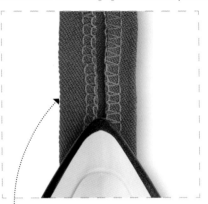

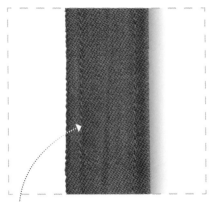

10 **For the belt carriers:** Neaten the edges of the belt carriers using a 3-thread overlock stitch or a small zigzag stitch.

11 **Fold the edges of the belt carriers** to the centre WS to WS and press.

12 Working from the RS (right side), **topstitch either side of the belt carrier**.

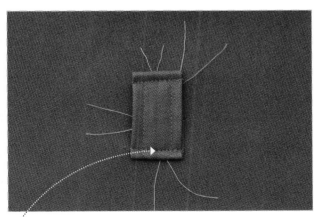

13 **Cut the belt carriers** to the length required to hold your belt. Fold the carriers into a loop and pin at the marked positions.

14 **Topstitch the top and bottom** of the belt carriers to secure. Remove the tailor's tacks.

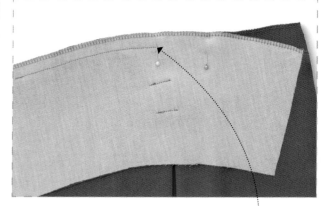

15 **Place the yoke** to the skirt front and back. Pin and machine. Press the seam open.

16 **Press the skirt-to-yoke seam** open, then neaten the side seams using a 3-thread overlock stitch or a small zigzag stitch.

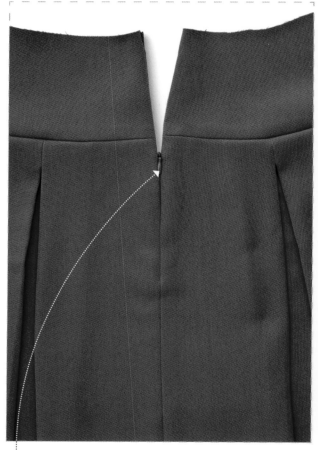

17 **Insert a zip** of your choice on the LH (left hand) side (see pp.24–25). Stitch the remainder of the side seam and press open.

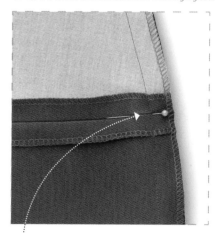

18 **Join the RH side seam,** matching at the skirt-to-yoke seam. Press open.

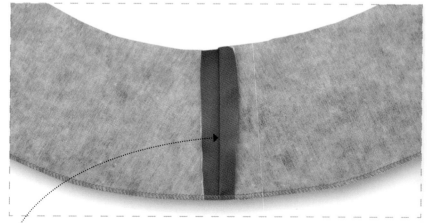

19 **Attach a lightweight interfacing** to the remaining set of yokes to make the yoke facings (see p.16). Join the facings at the RH side and press the seam open. Neaten the lower edge using either a 3-thread overlock stitch or a small zigzag stitch.

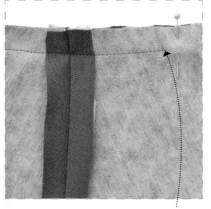

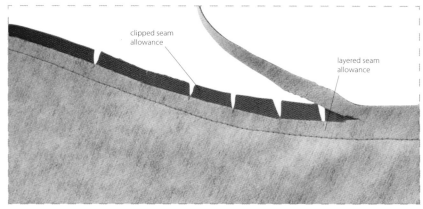

clipped seam
allowance

layered seam
allowance

20 **Place the yoke facing to the yoke** RS (right side) to RS, matching at the side seam. Pin and machine.

21 **Layer the seam allowance** by trimming the facing side of the seam to half its width. **Clip the seam allowance** to reduce bulk (see p.22).

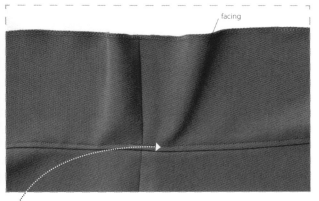

facing

22 **Press the seam** towards the facing and understitch (see p.23).

23 **Turn the facing to the inside** then fold the edge of the facing in to meet the zip tape. Pin. Pin the facing to the skirt-to-yoke seam.

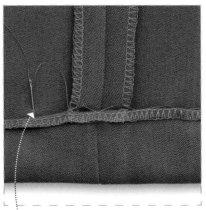

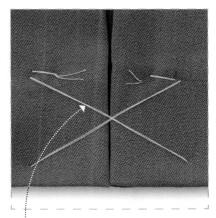

24 Working from the RS (right side) of the skirt **stitch in the ditch** – the line produced by the skirt-to-yoke seam – through all layers. This will secure the facing on the inside.

25 **Neaten the hem edge** (see pp.18–19). Turn up and handstitch in place. Remove the tacks in the pleats.

26 **Fold the pleats** at the hem edge back into place and tack together with a large X. Press. Remove any remaining tacks and trace tacks.

Dress Pattern One

CLASSIC WAISTED DRESS

This dress has a darted bodice fitted into the waist for a smooth, flattering line at the waist and hips. To make this dress with short sleeves, copy the sleeve pattern and mark the seamlines. Mark a point either side of the sleeve, 15cm (6in) below the armhole seamlines. Join these points to make a new hemline. Draw a new cutting line 1.5cm ($^5/_8$in) below the new hemline. It is recommended to make the pattern up in calico first to ensure a good fit.

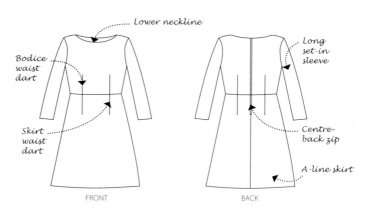

BEFORE YOU START

YOU WILL NEED

- 2.5m (98in) x 150cm (59in) fabric
- 1 x reel matching all-purpose sewing thread
- 1 x reel contrasting all-purpose sewing thread for pattern marking
- 50cm (20in) lightweight interfacing
- 1 x 56cm (22in) zip

PREPARING THE PATTERN

- This dress is made using Dress Pattern Two (see pp.56–57)
- Follow the instructions (see pp.48–49) to copy or download the pattern in your size

GARMENT CONSTRUCTION

This unlined two-piece dress has waist darts in the bodice and in the skirt. It has long, fitted set-in sleeves and a lower neckline finished with a facing. There is a zip in the centre back and the A-line skirt sits just on the knee.

Lower neckline

Bodice waist dart

Skirt waist dart

Long set-in sleeve

Centre-back zip

A-line skirt

FRONT

BACK

HOW TO MAKE THE CLASSIC WAISTED DRESS

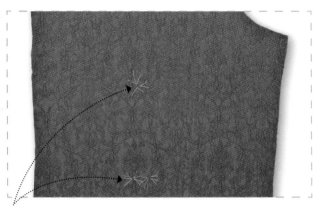

1 **Cut out the fabric and mark the darts** using tailor's tacks (see p.9).

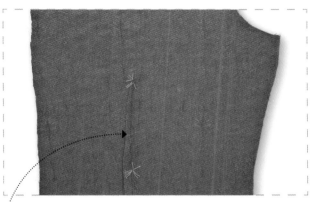

2 **Make all the darts** (see p.14) and press towards the centre of the garment.

3 **Join the front and back skirts to the front and back bodices,** matching the darts. To ensure they match, you may have to ease the skirt to the bodice by stretching the bodice slightly. Press the seam allowances together.

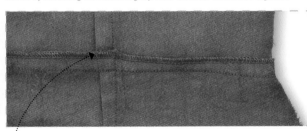

4 **Neaten the seam allowances** together using either a 3-thread overlock stitch or a small zigzag stitch (see p.13). Press up towards the bodice.

5 Using either a 3-thread overlock stitch or a small zigzag stitch, **neaten the CB (centre back) seam, the side seams, and the shoulder seams** on both the front and the back.

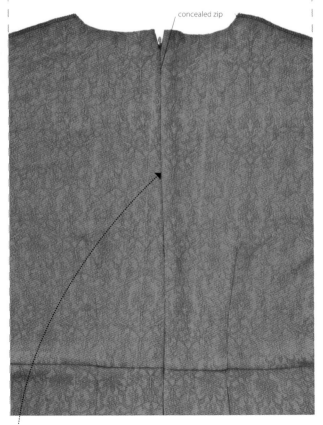

concealed zip

6 Making sure the waist seams match on either side, **insert a zip** of your choice in the CB (see pp.24–25). **Stitch the remainder of the CB seam** and press open.

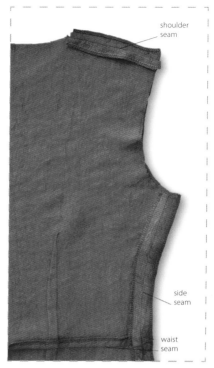

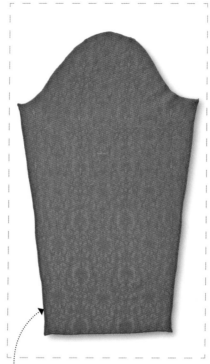

7 **Join the front to the back** at the shoulder and side seams, matching at the waist seam. Press the seams open.

8 **Neaten the sides and lower edge of both sleeves** using either a 3-thread overlock stitch or a small zigzag stitch.

9 **Machine the sleeve seam** and press open. Using stitch length 5, machine two rows of ease stitches through the sleeve head (see p.20).

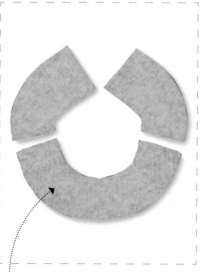

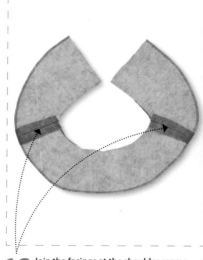

10 **Insert the sleeve** (see p.20) and neaten the raw edges using either a 3-thread overlock stitch or a small zigzag stitch.

11 **Attach a lightweight fusible interfacing** to the neck facing pieces (see p.16).

12 **Join the facings at the shoulder seams** and press the seams open. Neaten the lower edge using either a 3-thread overlock stitch or a small zigzag stitch.

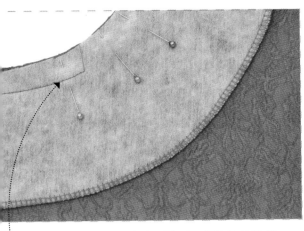

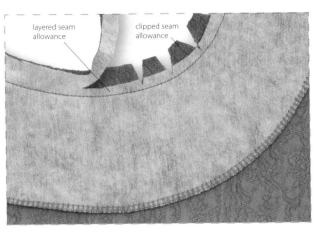

13 **Place the facings** to the neck edge of the dress RS (right side) to RS, matching the seams. Pin and machine.

14 **Layer the seam allowance** by trimming the facing side of the seam to half its width. **Clip the seam allowance** to reduce bulk.

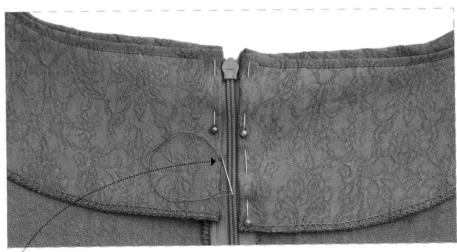

15 **Understitch the seam allowances** to the facing.

16 **Turn the facing to the inside** then, at the CB, **fold the edge of the facing** in to meet the zip tape. Pin and handstitch in place.

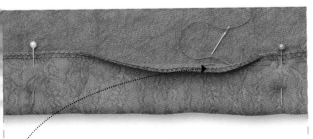

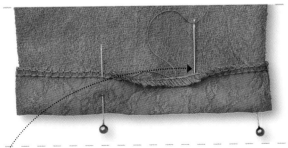

17 **Neaten the hem edge** (see pp.18–19) and turn up by 4cm (1½in). To ease the fullness out of the hem, **make a row of running stitches** close to the neatened edge. Pull the thread to tighten the fabric. Handstitch, then remove the running stitches.

18 **Turn up a 2.5cm (1in) hem** at the bottom of each sleeve. Pin and handstitch in place.

Dress Pattern Two

CLASSIC EMPIRE LINE DRESS

Those ladies of The First French Empire certainly knew a thing or two about how to flatter the figure. The high waist of an Empire Line Dress helps to conceal a fuller waistline and the low neck of this version sets off the face and neck. Choose your pattern size by your bust measurement and check for fit in the hip and waist areas. This is an easy-to-wear day dress that can take you from work to dinner.

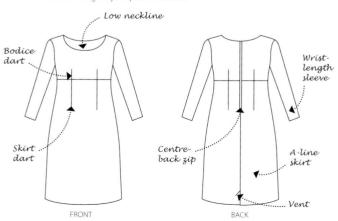

BEFORE YOU START

YOU WILL NEED

- 2.50m (98$\frac{1}{2}$in) x 150cm (59in) fabric
- 1 x reel matching all-purpose sewing thread
- 1 x reel contrasting all-purpose sewing thread for pattern marking
- 50cm (20in) lightweight interfacing
- 1 x 56cm (22in) zip

PREPARING THE PATTERN

- This dress is made using Dress Pattern Two (see pp.59–61)
- Follow the instructions (see pp.48–49) to copy or download the pattern in your size

GARMENT CONSTRUCTION

This unlined dress has wrist-length sleeves and a wide, low neckline finished with a facing. The waist darts of the bodice meet the skirt darts at an under-bust seamline. There is a centre back (CB) zip and a vent in the gently shaped A-line skirt.

Low neckline

Bodice dart

Skirt dart

FRONT

Centre-back zip

Wrist-length sleeve

A-line skirt

Vent

BACK

HOW TO MAKE THE CLASSIC EMPIRE LINE DRESS

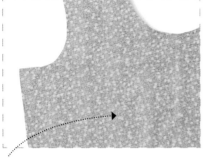

1 **Cut out the fabric** and mark the darts using tailor's tacks (see p9).

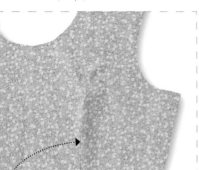

2 **Make the darts** (see p.14) in the bodice and skirt and press towards the centre of the garment.

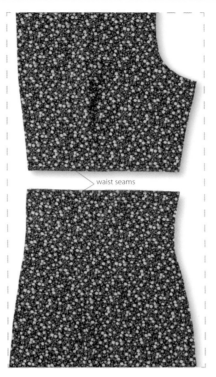

waist seams

3 **Neaten the waist seams** on all the bodice and skirt pieces using a 3-thread overlock stitch or a small zigzag stitch.

4 **Join the front bodice to the front skirt** and the back bodice pieces to the back skirts at the waist. Press the seams open.

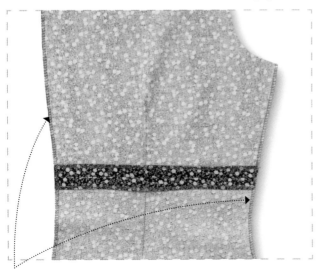

5 **Neaten all the side seams, shoulder seams, and the CB (centre back) seam** using a 3-thread overlock stitch or a small zigzag stitch.

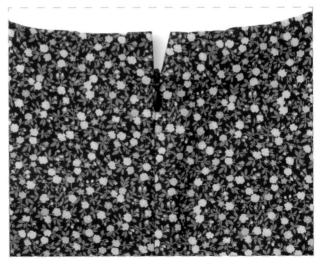

6 **Insert a zip** of your choice in the CB (see pp.24–25). Stitch the remainder of the CB seam stopping at the dot marking the top of the vent.

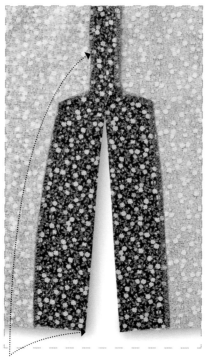

shoulder seam

side seam

7 Press the seam and the vent open.

8 Join the front to the back pieces at the shoulder and side seams. Press the seams open.

9 Neaten the sides and lower edge of both sleeves using either a 3-thread overlock stitch or a small zigzag stitch.

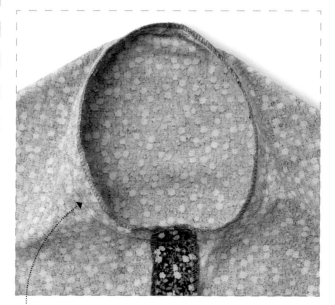

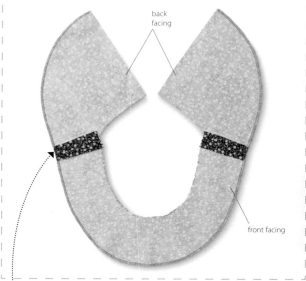

back facing

front facing

10 Machine the sleeve side seam and press it open. Using the longest stitch available, machine two rows of ease stitches through the sleeve head (see p.20). Fit the sleeve into the armhole, RS (right side) to RS. Pin, then stitch the sleeve into place from the sleeve side (see p.20).

11 Attach a lightweight fusible interfacing to the neck facing pieces (see p.16). Join the facings at the shoulder seams and press the seams open. Neaten the lower edge of the facing pieces (see p.17).

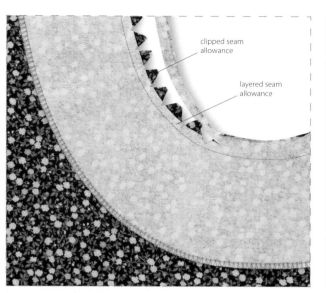

clipped seam allowance

layered seam allowance

12 **Place the facings to the neck edge of the dress** RS to RS, matching the seams. Pin and machine. **Layer the seam allowance** by trimming the facing side of the seam to half its width. **Clip the seam allowance** to reduce bulk (see p.22).

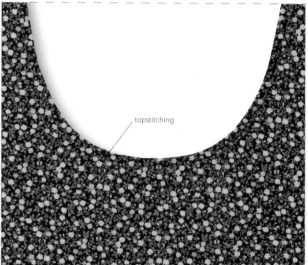

topstitching

13 **Turn the facing to the WS** (wrong side), press and topstitch to hold in place.

hem edge

mitre

14 **Neaten the hem edge.** On each side of the vent, **remove the surplus fabric** in the hem allowance. Mitre the hem at the bottom of the vent and pin. Turn up the remainder of the hem and pin. Handstitch the mitre and hem in place.

15 **Turn up the sleeve hem** by 3cm (1¹/₂in), pin and handstitch in place.

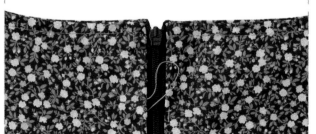

16 At the CB, **fold the edge of the facing in to meet the zip tape.** Pin and handstitch in place.

USING THE PATTERN SECTION

To create any of the garments in this book, you will first need to transfer the pattern to paper. You can do this in one of two ways: draw the pattern by hand onto pattern paper, or enlarge it on a photocopier. Before you begin, you will also need to find the correct size for you.

FIND YOUR SIZE

Find your size by taking your bust, waist, and hip measurements and finding the closest set of measurements in the table below. If you are between sizes, choose the larger of the two.

Size	6–8	8–10	10–12	12–14	14–16	16–18	18–20	20–22	22–24
Bust	82cm (32¼in)	84.5cm (33¼in)	87cm (34¼in)	92cm (36¼in)	97cm (38in)	102cm (40in)	107cm (42in)	112cm (44in)	117cm (46in)
Waist	62cm (24½in)	64.5cm (25¼in)	67cm (26¼in)	72cm (28¼in)	77cm (30¼in)	82cm (32¼in)	87cm (34¼in)	92cm (36¼in)	97cm (38in)
Hip	87cm (34¼in)	89.5cm (35¼in)	92cm (36¼in)	97cm (38in)	102cm (40in)	107cm (42in)	112cm (44in)	117cm (46in)	122cm (48in)

VARIED SIZES

You may have noticed that your size in the table differs from what you would buy in a store.

In general, dressmaking sizes tend to be smaller than store sizes.

SEAM ALLOWANCE

Seam allowance is the amount of fabric that is taken up by the seam. It is usually given as the distance between the cutting line and the stitching line.

The patterns in this section include 1.5cm (⁵⁄₈in) seam allowance. This means that to make a garment that is the correct size and shape, you will need to cut along the line on the pattern, and stitch 1.5cm (⁵⁄₈in) inside the cutting line. An easy way to remember to do this is to mark a stitching line onto the pattern pieces before you begin.

Cutting line

Stitching line

PATTERN MARKINGS

The following markings are used on the patterns in this section.

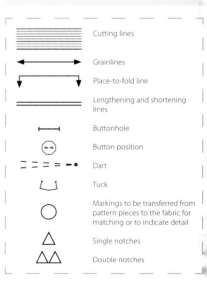

≡≡≡	Cutting lines
◄─────►	Grainlines
▼───▼	Place-to-fold line
───	Lengthening and shortening lines
├───┤	Buttonhole
⊙	Button position
⌐ ⌐ = = ─ •	Dart
⊔	Tuck
○	Markings to be transferred from pattern pieces to the fabric for matching or to indicate detail
△	Single notches
△△	Double notches

SIMPLE PATTERN ALTERATIONS

t everyone is lucky enough to be a "stock size". You may be short or tall, or your ms or legs may be longer than a pattern allows. If any of these are true of you, u will need to shorten or lengthen the pattern before you cut out your fabric. s easy to shorten or lengthen a long sleeve: to shorten, all you need to do is off the required amount at the hem of the pattern – as shown on the Classic ft dress and the Classic waisted dress. To lengthen, work out the amount you nt to lengthen by, cut a band of paper to this width, and tape it to the hem of e pattern. Trim away any excess paper along the sides of the pattern to give a ooth, continuous line.

busers are a little more complicated as you need to retain the correct width over e hips. For that reason, you should make length adjustments midway between e hip and the hem. Measure then mark this lengthening/shortening line on the ttern piece. To shorten at this point, work out the amount you want to shorten

by and mark this amount at intervals above your shortening line. Using a ruler as a guide, draw a line through your marks, then fold the lengthening/shortening line onto the drawn line so the two lines meet neatly, forming a pleat in the pattern. Press the pleat down firmly and secure it with tape. To lengthen at this point, work out the amount you want to lengthen by. Carefully cut through the lengthening/ shortening line on your pattern piece. Place some paper behind the pattern and spread the pattern pieces apart to leave a gap of the required amount. Make sure the gap is even all the way along. Tape the pattern pieces to the paper and trim away any excess paper along the sides of the pattern piece so you have a smooth, continuous line.

If you are altering a skirt or dress pattern, do make sure to alter the front and back pattern pieces by the same amount and along lengthening/shortening lines that are at the same distance from the hem on both pattern pieces.

COPY YOUR PATTERN

METHOD 1: DRAWING THE PATTERN BY HAND

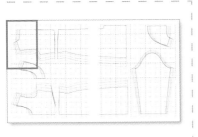 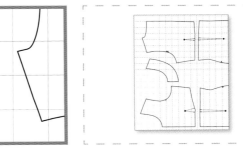

1 Each grid square in the patterns represents a 5cm square at full size. To enlarge the patterns y hand, you will need pattern paper with either a :m (¹/₂in) or 5cm (2in) grid.

2 Begin by finding the coloured line for your size in the pattern. Enlarge the pattern onto your paper, mapping each square of the pattern onto a 5cm square on the pattern paper.

3 Depending on the size of your pattern paper, you may need to stick together several sheets to fit all the pieces for a single pattern. Once you have copied all the pieces, cut them out.

METHOD 2: PHOTOCOPYING

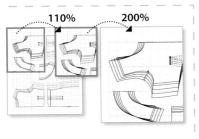 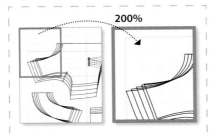 

1 To enlarge the pattern on a photocopier, begin by copying it at 110%. Find your size in the able, and draw along the line for your size in marker or pen. Enlarge the pattern by 200%.

2 Enlarge the pattern pieces again by 200% to reach full size. If you are using a photocopier that has a 400% setting, you can use this setting to enlarge the pieces in one step.

3 Once you have enlarged all parts of the original page, piece them together using the gridlines as a guide, and tape them down. Cut around your size.

SKIRT PATTERN ONE

FOLD

SKIRT BACK
Cut 1 on folded fabric

WAISTBAND
Cut 1

CB

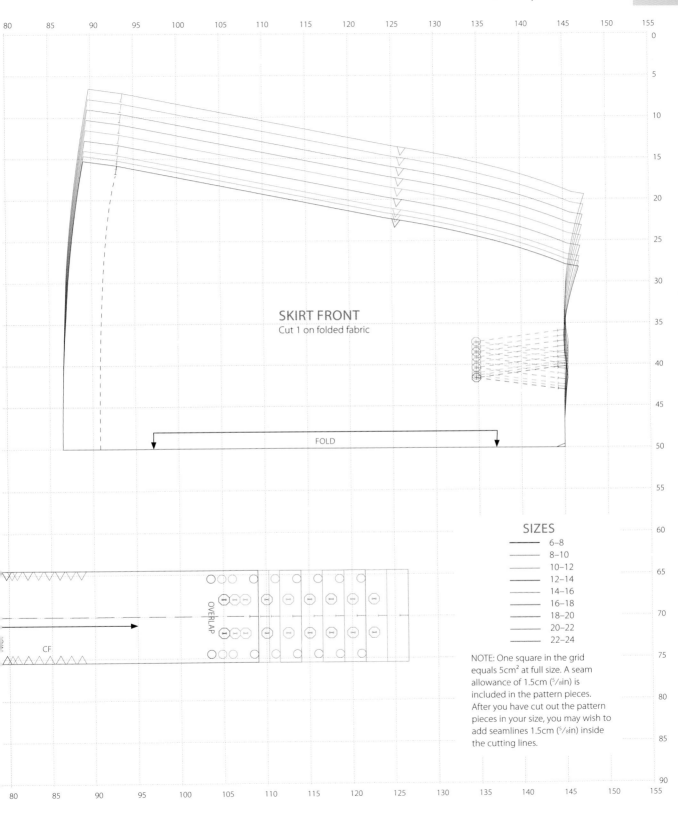

SKIRT FRONT
Cut 1 on folded fabric

FOLD

OVERLAP

CF

SIZES

——	6–8
——	8–10
——	10–12
——	12–14
——	14–16
——	16–18
——	18–20
——	20–22
——	22–24

NOTE: One square in the grid equals 5cm² at full size. A seam allowance of 1.5cm (⅝in) is included in the pattern pieces. After you have cut out the pattern pieces in your size, you may wish to add seamlines 1.5cm (⅝in) inside the cutting lines.

SKIRT PATTERN TWO

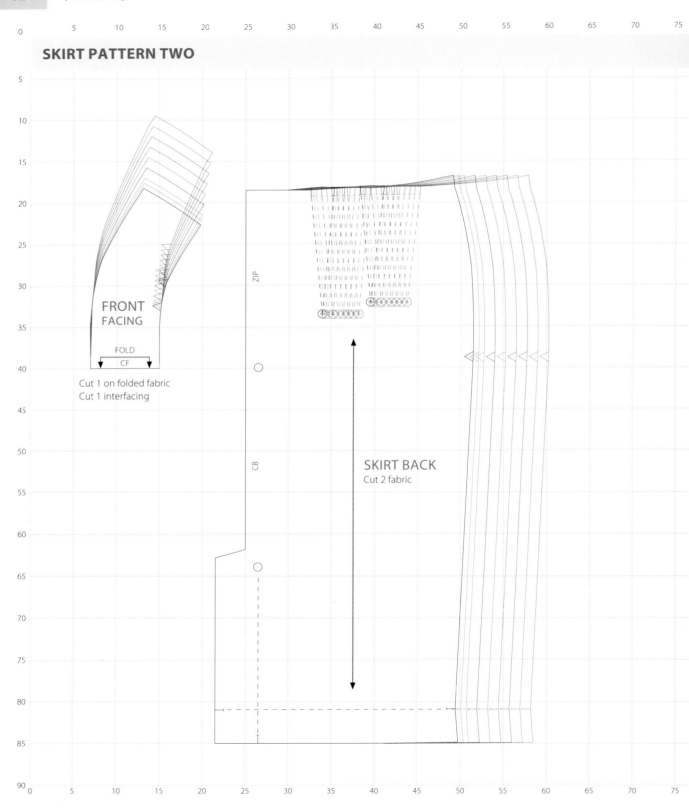

FRONT
FACING

FOLD
CF

Cut 1 on folded fabric
Cut 1 interfacing

ZIP

CB

SKIRT BACK
Cut 2 fabric

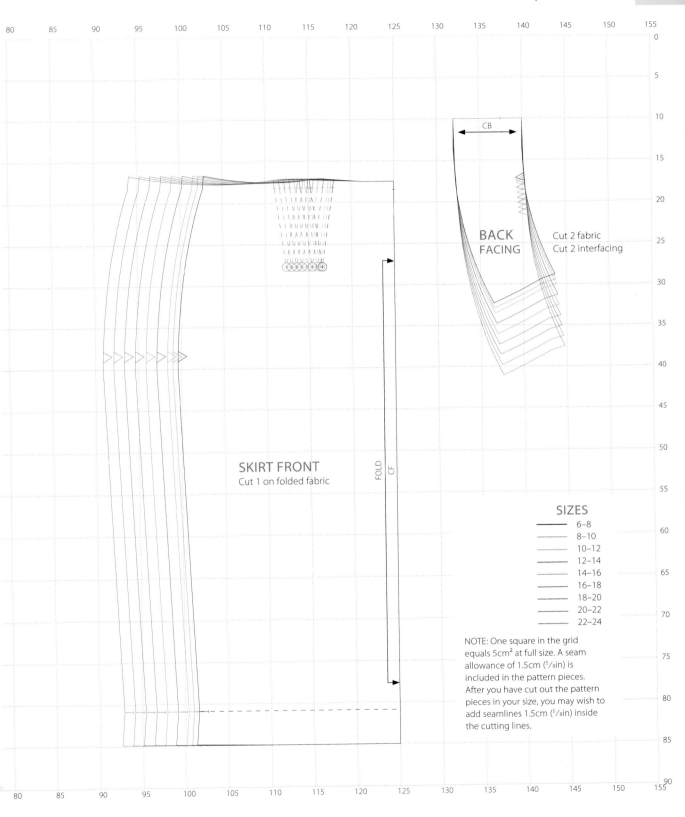

BACK FACING

Cut 2 fabric
Cut 2 interfacing

CB

SKIRT FRONT
Cut 1 on folded fabric

FOLD
CF

SIZES

——	6–8
——	8–10
——	10–12
——	12–14
——	14–16
——	16–18
——	18–20
——	20–22
——	22–24

NOTE: One square in the grid equals 5cm² at full size. A seam allowance of 1.5cm (⁵/₈in) is included in the pattern pieces. After you have cut out the pattern pieces in your size, you may wish to add seamlines 1.5cm (⁵/₈in) inside the cutting lines.

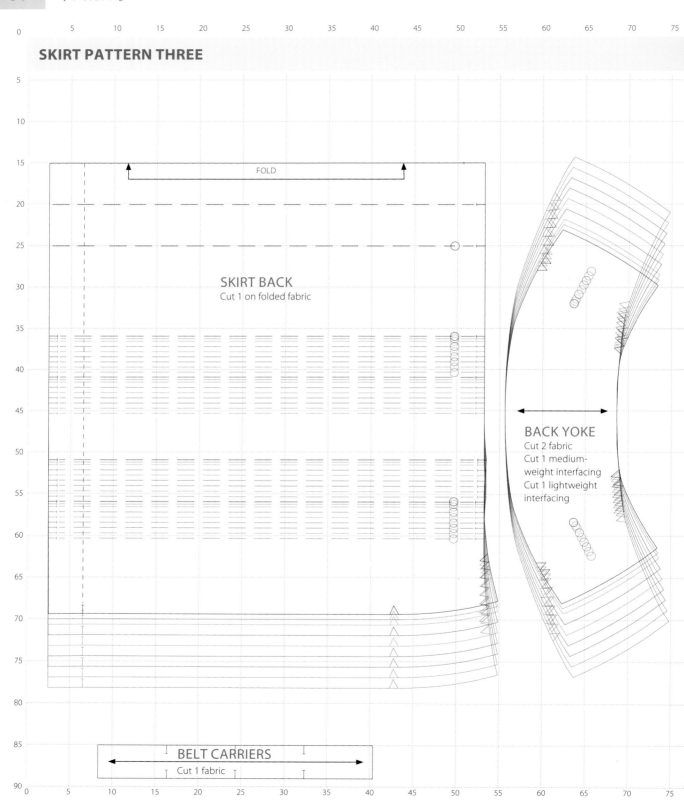

SKIRT PATTERN THREE

FOLD

SKIRT BACK
Cut 1 on folded fabric

BACK YOKE
Cut 2 fabric
Cut 1 medium-
weight interfacing
Cut 1 lightweight
interfacing

BELT CARRIERS
Cut 1 fabric

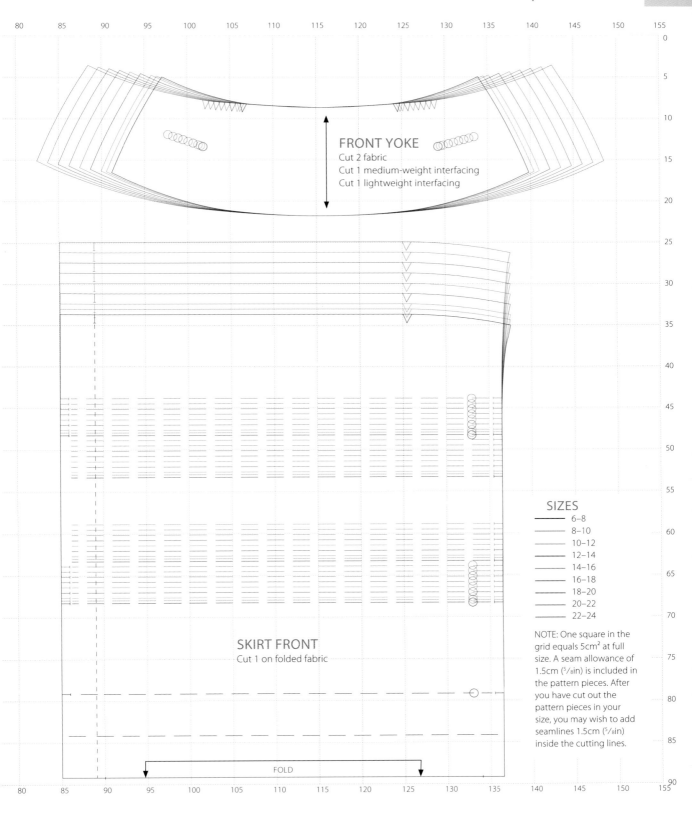

FRONT YOKE
Cut 2 fabric
Cut 1 medium-weight interfacing
Cut 1 lightweight interfacing

SKIRT FRONT
Cut 1 on folded fabric

FOLD

SIZES
— 6–8
— 8–10
— 10–12
— 12–14
— 14–16
— 16–18
— 18–20
— 20–22
— 22–24

NOTE: One square in the grid equals 5cm² at full size. A seam allowance of 1.5cm (⁵⁄₈in) is included in the pattern pieces. After you have cut out the pattern pieces in your size, you may wish to add seamlines 1.5cm (⁵⁄₈in) inside the cutting lines.

DRESS PATTERN ONE

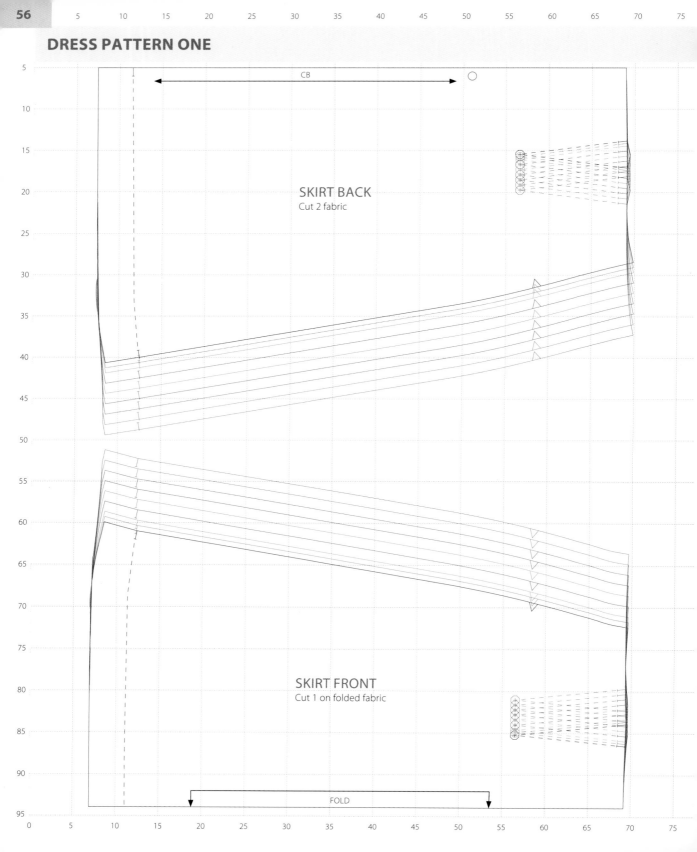

CB

SKIRT BACK
Cut 2 fabric

SKIRT FRONT
Cut 1 on folded fabric

FOLD

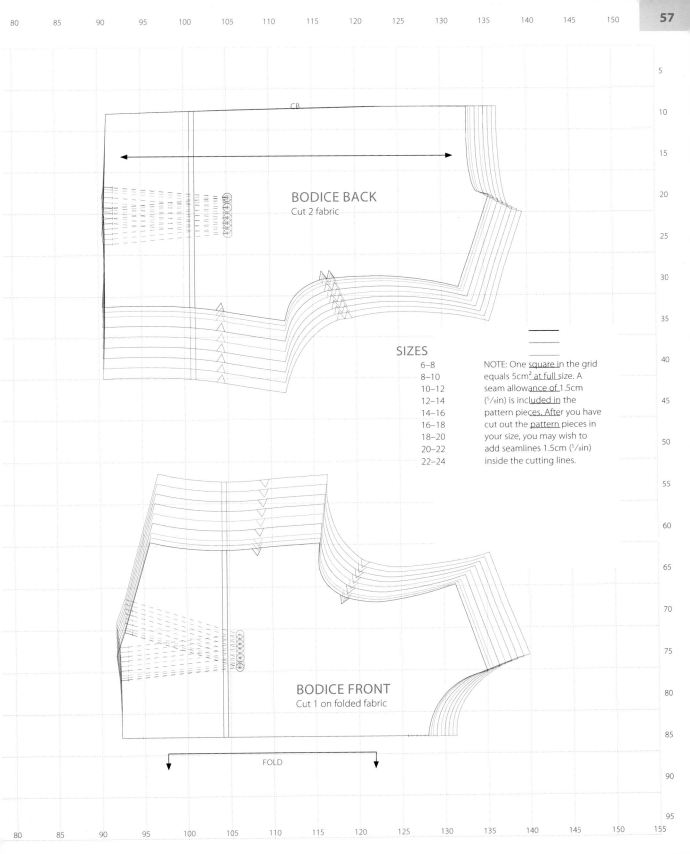

BODICE BACK
Cut 2 fabric

SIZES
6–8
8–10
10–12
12–14
14–16
16–18
18–20
20–22
22–24

NOTE: One square in the grid equals 5cm² at full size. A seam allowance of 1.5cm (⅝in) is included in the pattern pieces. After you have cut out the pattern pieces in your size, you may wish to add seamlines 1.5cm (⅝in) inside the cutting lines.

BODICE FRONT
Cut 1 on folded fabric

FOLD

CB

SLEEVE
Cut 2 fabric

FRONT
FACING

FOLD

Cut 1 on folded fabric
Cut 1 on folded interfacing

BACK
FACING

CB

Cut 2 fabric
Cut 2 interfacing

DRESS PATTERN TWO

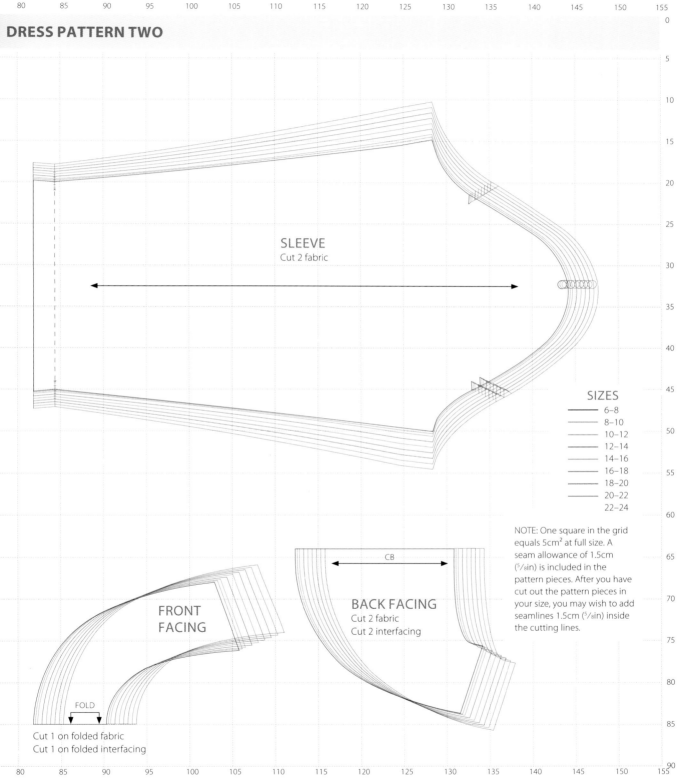

80 85 90 95 100 105 110 115 120 125 130 135 140 145 150 155

SLEEVE
Cut 2 fabric

SIZES
— 6–8
— 8–10
— 10–12
— 12–14
— 14–16
— 16–18
— 18–20
— 20–22
— 22–24

NOTE: One square in the grid equals 5cm² at full size. A seam allowance of 1.5cm (⁵⁄₈in) is included in the pattern pieces. After you have cut out the pattern pieces in your size, you may wish to add seamlines 1.5cm (⁵⁄₈in) inside the cutting lines.

FRONT FACING

Cut 1 on folded fabric
Cut 1 on folded interfacing

FOLD

CB

BACK FACING
Cut 2 fabric
Cut 2 interfacing

80 85 90 95 100 105 110 115 120 125 130 135 140 145 150 155

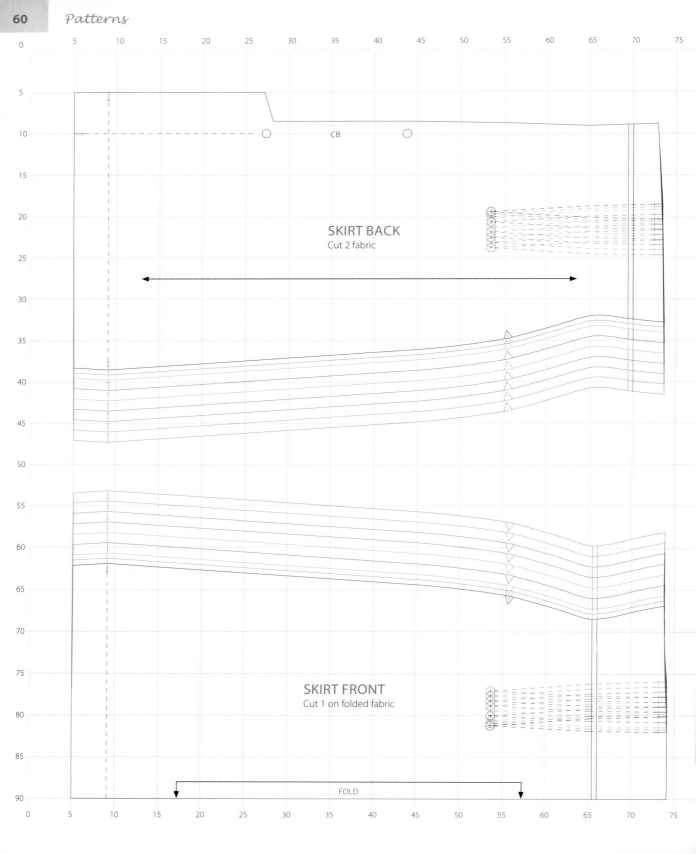

SKIRT BACK
Cut 2 fabric

CB

SKIRT FRONT
Cut 1 on folded fabric

FOLD

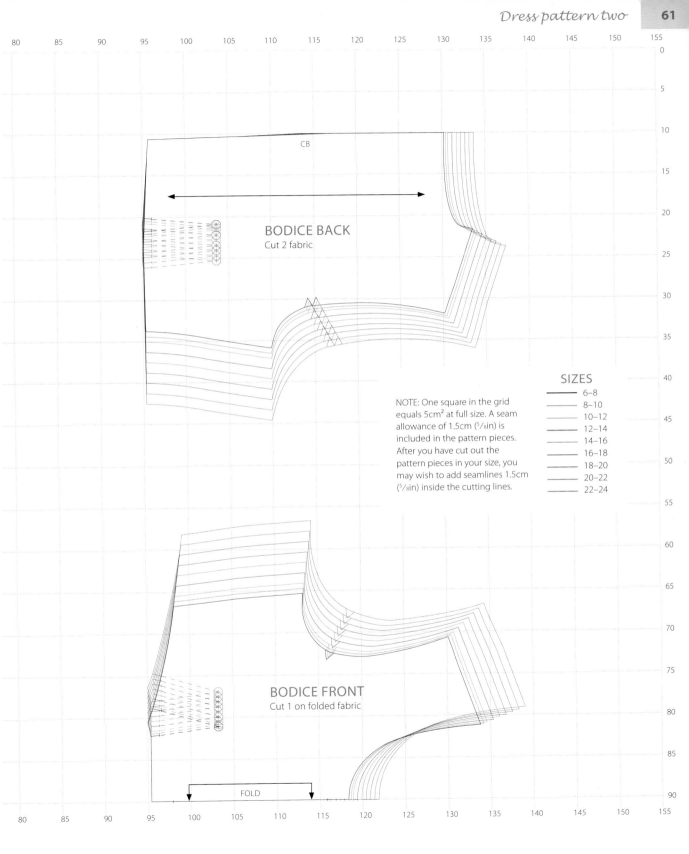

CB

BODICE BACK
Cut 2 fabric

BODICE FRONT
Cut 1 on folded fabric

FOLD

NOTE: One square in the grid equals 5cm² at full size. A seam allowance of 1.5cm (⁵⁄₈in) is included in the pattern pieces. After you have cut out the pattern pieces in your size, you may wish to add seamlines 1.5cm (⁵⁄₈in) inside the cutting lines.

SIZES
6–8
8–10
10–12
12–14
14–16
16–18
18–20
20–22
22–24

INDEX

ABOUT THE AUTHOR

Alison Smith trained as an Art and Fashion Textile Teacher before becoming Head of Textiles at one of the largest secondary schools in Birmingham. Alison left mainstream teaching to have a family, but missed teaching so much that she soon established the Alison Victoria School of Sewing. The school is now the largest of its kind in the UK with students attending from all over Europe and beyond. Alison specialises not only in teaching Dressmaking but also Tailoring and Corsetry. In addition to her own school, Alison lectures at Janome in Stockport, and various sewing shows across the UK. Alison has brought her passion for sewing to TV on series such as *From Ladette to Lady*. Alison lives in Leicestershire with her husband Nigel and has two adult children.

ACKNOWLEDGMENTS

AUTHOR'S ACKNOWLEDGMENTS

No book could ever be written without a little help. I would like to thank the following people for their help in making all the garments: Jackie Boddy, Averil Wing, Jenny Holdam, Christine Scott, Angela Paine, and Joan Culver. My darling husband Nigel and our children Kathryn and Oliver for all their support and endless cups of tea! Thanks must also go to the companies who have continued to support me: Janome UK, Coats Crafts, Fruedenberg –nw, Fabulous Fabric, and MIG. Thank you to my editors Laura Palosuo and Hilary Mandleberg.

DK would like to thank Hilary Mandleberg for compiling this book and writing additional text.

DK ACKNOWLEDGMENTS

DK would like to thank all the people who helped in the creation of this book: Alison Shackleton for art direction, and Paula Keogh for her skills as sewing technician on the first photo shoot; Jane Ewart for art direction on the second photo shoot, Ruth Jenkinson and her assistant Carly for photography, and Rebecca Fallowfield for production assistance. We are immensely grateful to our models Kate and Charlotte. A big thank you goes out to Bob at MIG for demystifying the art of pattern creation. Finally, we would like to thank Claire Cross for editorial assistance, Ria Holland for design assistance, Angela Baynham for proofreading, and Marie Lorimer for indexing.